Łukasz Gładysiak • Mike Koenig • Jacek

Königstiger

KAGERO

Königstiger • Łukasz Gładysiak • Mike Koenig • Jacek Szafrański
• First edition • LUBLIN 2014

© All English Language Rights Reserved. With the exception of quoting brief passages for the purposes of review, no part of this publication may be reproduced without prior written permission from the Publisher. Nazwa serii zastrzeżona w UP RP • **ISBN 978-83-64596-23-0**

Editors: **Łukasz Gładysiak, Marek Jaszczołt** • Translation: **Łukasz Gładysiak** • Color profiles: **Arkadiusz Wróbel**
• Scale drawings: **Mariusz Suliga**
• Design: **KAGERO STUDIO, Marcin Wachowicz**

Oficyna Wydawnicza KAGERO
Akacjowa 100, Turka, os. Borek, 20-258 Lublin 62, Poland, phone/fax: (+48) 81 501 21 05
www.kagero.pl • e-mail: kagero@kagero.pl, marketing@kagero.pl
w w w . k a g e r o . p l

Nowadays *Panzerkampfwagen VI Ausführung B* heavy tanks are regarded by many as a synonym for the highest power of the German *Panzerwaffe* of World War Two. Nearly 70-ton giants, armed with powerful 88 mm caliber main gun has really wreaked terror in the ranks of the allied coalition soldiers. The problem was, however, in that it produced in quantities of less than half a thousand copies, so called *King Tigers* were not able to reverse the dramatic situation in which the Third Reich had been, when they were put into service more. Nevertheless, these vehicles have become one of the armored legends not only the last of the world wars, but for the whole of the twentieth century.

Construction History

The origins of the tanks, which today is called *Königstiger* (in English: *King* or *Royal Tiger*), dates back to the autumn of 1942. It was then, the German Land Forces Armament Office (*Heereswaffenamt*) officials commissioned *Henschel und Sohn Aktiengesellschaft* of Kassel to develop a new heavy tank, which had been to implement *Panzerkampfwagen VI Ausf. E* – the tanks that were put into service nearly that time. The basic guidelines associated with the new type of armored vehicle were very thick, because reaching up to 180 mm armor and already developed *8.8 cm Kampfwagenkanone 43 L / 71 (Gerät 5-0808)* 88-milimeters tank gun. In January of the following year builders were suggested to have planned tank components unified as much as possible with, also being developed at this time by *Maschinenfabrik Augsburg Nürnberg*, a new type of medium tank, but rather, using actual terminology - the main tank, *Panzerkampfwagen V Panther Ausführung F*. At this time, the conceptual work on a new heavy tank included also company located in St. Valentin, *Nibelungenwerke Aktiengesellschaft*.

The Austrian company was not only which management had been counting on lucrative contracts related to the new version of the famous *Tiger*. The constructor team centered around the creator, inter alia, *Volkswagena Beetle*, Professor Ferdinand Porsche, presented their own proposal to *Heereswaffenamt* representatives too. Their vehicle, which in fact was the modernized version of a competitive for *Pz.Kpfw. VI Ausf. E*, so-called *Porsche Tiger* was designated *Verschuskonstruktion 4501 Porsche - VK 4501 (P)*. The Professor's team was intended to create prototypes in two versions: with a turret installed closer to the front edge of the hull (the idea taken from a Soviet tank *T-34*) and placed in the back in such a way that the engine compartment separated the driver and radio operator from the other crew members in similar manner to *Ferdinand/Elefant* self-propelled gun. Turrets for both variants: Henschel and Porsche, were in fact designed and subsequently produced in the factories of *Krupp Aktiengesellschaft* in Essen.

In mid-January 1943 new German heavy tank models that June 2nd was designated *Panzerkampfwagen VI Ausführung B* (*Sonderkraftfahrzeug 182*, earlier the vehicle was determined as *H3 Tiger* or *Tiger II*), were presented to Adolf Hitler. The *Führer* decided that the contest winner was the *Henschel* factory team, and this plant was instructed to prepare three prototypes. A full-size wooden mock-up was revealed on 20 October 1943 at Orzysz proving ground in East Prussia, now in Poland (*Truppenübungsplatz Arys*). Prototypes were completed in Kassel in November (*V1* number) and December (*V2* and *V3* numbers).

At the end of the fifth year of the war the contest-winning factory received orders for more than 1,200 new heavy tanks. The production were based on the cooperation of No. III *Henschel* Factory and *Wegmann & Company* plant, both located in the same city over Fulda. In the coming weeks the plan was corrected several times, oscillating altogether within 1,500 exemplars. One of the production plans stated the four series re-

Photo set of *Panzerkampfwagen VI Ausf. B* with *Porsche* turret (tactical number: 11) *Funklenk-Panzer-Kompanie 316* which was a part of *Panzer-Lehr-Division* during the Normandy Campaign, abandoned by its crew on Châteaudun on June 17, 1944. This vehicle, as well as five other *Königstiger* tanks were captured by the *US Army* soldiers. The wrecks were finally collected in the beginning of fifties. The unusual but characteristic for this unit tactical number is clearly visible. [Kagero Archive]

spectively of 176, 350, 379 and 329 vehicles in each. Ultimately, as indicated by Thomas Jentz, the average monthly production were to reach fifty tanks.

In fact, because of the increasingly afflict the Third Reich problems with the delivery of raw materials and armaments production rate, as well as harassing German industrial centers by the Allied bombing (during several conducted, among others, 22 and 27 September and 7 October and 15 December 1944, in Kassel production halls were destroyed several almost ready *Königstiger*), in the period from January 1944 to March 1945 489 and three prototypes were completed (including 377 exemplars in 1944). It is estimated that because of the bombing raids, the Germans failed to finish the next nearly 660 vehicles. The chassis number of the first of production series *Royal Tigers* was 280,001. The confirmed number of *Pz.Kpfw. VI Ausf. B* heavy tanks manufactured in 1944 and 1945 could be found in Table 1.

Table 1. *Pz.Kpfw. VI Ausf. B* heavy tank monthly production

1944

I	II	III	IV	V	VI	VII	VIII	IX	X	XI	XII
3	5	6	6	15	32	45	84	73	26	35	47

Total: 377 vehicles

1945

I	II	III
40	42	30

Total: 112 vehicles

During the 14-months production period, *Pz.Kpfw. VI Ausf. B* underwent a number of modifications. These included for example the shape of fenders, the deployment of elements on

the upper armor of the engine compartment and to supplement that part of the hull, especially in the case of vehicles designed for operations on the western front, with additional protective shields of inter alia air intakes. It was also decided to remove the installation for deep fording device, present in case of exemplars manufactured before June 1944. The shape of the tow hitch was also adjusted as well as U-shaped sight aperture protection installed. Inside a fundamental change was the replacement of binocular *Turmzielfernrohr 9b/1* sighting telescope with monocular *TZF 9d* one. In the course of production mechanisms of the main armament also been improved development, creating the *8.8 cm KWK 43/II* and *8.8 cm KWK 43/III* variants. It is worth noting that beyond the stage of conceptual idea, retooling the *King Tiger* with 105-milimeters gun did not come. The main modifications of described vehicle and the month of their introduction could be found in Table 2.

The most noticeable difference between the first fifty exemplars of *Pz.Kpfw. VI Ausf. B* and other production series tanks was their turret. Initial series were equipped with a variant termed today as a *Porsche Model* (actually designed and manufactured by *Krupp AG* on the basis of a contract concluded in January 1943., designated *P2-Turm*), characterized by a clearly rounded front part, the commander cupola extending beyond the contour of the left side of the turret and a circular hole for throwing out the 88-milimeters shells. As an author of issued in 1999 encyclopedia of German armored vehicles, Peter Chamberlain suggests, it very quickly turned out that the front plate of this variant was more vulnerable to direct hits. The final choice was therefore called the *Henschel Model* turret (also developed by Krupp factories, called *H3-Turm* or *Serienturm*), with straight, 180 mm thick front plate and the 100-milimeters thick, cast gun mantlet equipped similar in shape to *Saukopfsblende*

(*the boar head*) installed for instance in self-propelled or assault guns. The *Henschel Model* turret became the standard one from June 1944, starting from the tank with a 280048 chassis number.

In November 1944 Kassel *Wegmann & Co.* factory acceded to convert regular production vehicles on the command versions, known as *Panzerbefehlslwagen mit 8,8 cm Kampfwagenkanone 43 L / 71*. The modification consisted in this case of the installation of additional radio set – *Funkgerätsatz 7* (vehicle designation: *Sonderkraftfahrzeug 268*) and *Funkgerätsatz 8* (*Sd.Kfz. 267*) in place of a part of ammunition stowage as well as an additional antenna socket on the outside of the tower, which allows for the installation of the characteristic so-called star antenna – *Sternantenne*. According to this modification, the telegraphic communication *Königstiger* units increased up to 80 km.

It should be recalled that a few months after the start of serial production of a new *Panzerwaffe* heavy tank, the production of a new variant of heavy tank destroyer based on the *Royal Tiger* chassis started too. The vehicle armed with 12.8 cm Panzerabwehrkanone 44 L/55 main gun and equipped with up to 250 mm thickness front armor, known as *Jagdpanzer VI Jagdtiger*, were produced in about 85 exemplars between July 1944 and March 1945. It is not the subject of this study.

Panzerkampfwagen VI. Ausf. B of the 2nd Company *schwere SS Panzer Abteilung 501* lost in Stavelot, December 1944. Its commander was SS-Oberscharfuhrer Kurt Sowa. [Kagero Archive]

US Army **armored unit soliders posing with** *Panzerkampfwagen VI Ausf. B* **of the 3rd Company** *schwere Heeres Panzer Abteilung 511* **abandoned in the Rengershausen area, spring 1945.** [Kagero Archive]

Table 2. *Pz.Kpfw. VI Ausf. B* **heavy tank modifications with the month of their implementation**

January 1944	Curved front fenders.
	Applying of *Zimmerit* anti-magnetic coat.
February 1944	Installing of *Tiger I* exhaust pipes.
	Installing of engine coolant heater with blow-torch access port.
May 1944	Installing of *Kgs 24/800/300* tracks.
	Installing of monocular *TZF 9d* sighting telescope.
	Installing of tow-piece main armament barrel.
June 1944	Deleting of deep fording device on the engine deck.
	Installing of three *Pilzen* sockets for a 2 t jib boom on the turret roof.
	Installing of the 40 mm thick loaders hatch instead of 15 mm one.
July 1944	Installing of track hangers on the turret sides.
August 1944	Adopting of the new model of 660 mm wide transport tracks.
	Interior painted with the red oxide primer instead of a white paint.
September 1944	*Zimmerit* anti-magnetic coat was no longer applied.
	Installing of the protective plate of the fuel intake.
October 1944	*Pilzen* sockets for a 2 t jib boom was no longer installed.
November 1944	Installing of the sighting telescopes' raincovers.
December 1944	Installing of air intake protective plates.
March 1945	Installing of *Kgs 73/800/152* tracks.
	Installing of the 18-teeth driving sprocket.

US Army **soldiers examining** *Panzerkampfwagen VI Ausf. B* **of** *schwere Heeres Panzer Abteilung 506* **near Schmallenberg, spring 1945.** [Kagero Archive]

Technical description

The power unit of *Panzerkampfwagen VI Ausführung B* heavy tank was petrol, liquid-cooled, line V 12 *Maybach HL 230 P30* engine with a capacity of 700 hp at 3000 rpm./min, embedded in a block made of aluminum. Its producer were *Maybach Motorenwerke* in Friedrichshafen and *Auto-Union Gesellschaft mit beschränkter Haftung* in Chemnitz. The one-off fuel, the standard *Wehrmacht* petrol with the octane of 74, supply was 830 l. It was transported it in six internal tanks to the smallest of which the crew members could have poured 65 liters and the largest: 170 l. Average *King Tiger* fuel consumption when driving on the road was about 650 l/100 km. While maneuvering in the field, this value could be increased up to 1000 liters. Proper lubrication of the drive unit provided a 40 liters of *Wehrmacht Motorenöl* oil.

According to the manufacturer, the vehicle maximum speed was 35 km/h. The tank driver could choose one of eight, offered by the *Maybach Olvar EG 40 12 16 Modell B* transmission, gears for forward and four reverse. Speeds achieved on individual ratios are given in Table 3.

The same vehicle seen from another angle. Note the remnants of foliage installed on the 88 mm barrel. [Kagero Archive]

Table 3. *Pz.Kpfw. VI Ausf. B* heavy tank maximum speed on individual gear ratios

Gear:	I	II	III	IV	V	VI	VII	VIII	Reverse (average)
Maximum speed [km/h]:	2,6	3,8	5,6	8,3	12,8	19,0	27,3	35,0	3,4

The *Royal Tiger* chassis consisted of nine pairs of solid steel wheels having a diameter of 800 mm and a width of 95 mm, without the rubber bandages cushioned independently installed on the torsion bar on each side. These elements supplied *Dianamaschinenfabrik* from Kassel. The presented vehicle used two types of tracks, connected with a 24 mm in diameter steel pins. The first, designated as *Kgs 73/660/52* with a width of 660 mm was mounted during the railway transport and the march of paved roads. Wider, *Kgs 73/800/52* were called the combat or battle variant. Since May 1944 it was replaces by *Kgs 24/800/300* version, which does not require a separate selection, directional links to the left and right sides.

Pz.Kpfw. VI Ausf. B armor was formed of steel chrome-vanadium (due to the loss of sources of supply of raw materials, from 1943 German steel mills began to resign from the admixture of molybdenum) plates with its surface hardened by carburizing. Their producer was the number of plants located within the boundaries of the Adolf Hitler country, including

Panzerkampfwagen VI Ausf. B with *Henschel* turret destroyed probably somewhere in Germany, Spring 1945. Despite it was hard to tow this colossus vehice, the towing V-shaped rod connected with front armor hooks of this *Königstiger* is clearly visible. [Kagero Archive]

French civilians and US Army soldiers posing with the *Panzerkampfwagen VI Ausf. B* with *Porsche* turret (tactical number: 11) of *Funklenk-Panzer-Kompanie 316* abandoned by its crew probably on June 19, 1944 near Janville in Normandy. There is a part of the characteristic, big tactical number of this German unit visible on the turret. [Kagero Archive]

but not limited *Eisenwerke Oberdonau* in Linz (Austria), *Skoda* in Hradec Kralove (nowadays Czech Republic), or, most likely, *Oberschlesische Hüttenwerk Malapane* that is Huta Mała Panew in Ozimek (Poland) today. The armor plates were combined by welding. Their thickness ranged from 25 to 150 mm in the case of the chassis and from 40 to 180 mm for the turret. These values, together with the angle of slope of the various parts of the armor are listed in Table 3.

In addition to armor greatest asset of *Pz.Kpfw. VI Ausf. B* was its main armament. Developed by Krupp AG concern the 8.8 cm Kampfwagenkanone 43 L/71 88-milimeters tank gun were among the most effective types of weapons that class during

One of the last production series *Panzerkampfwagen VI Ausf. B* with *Henschel* turret (manufactured probably in March 1945), abandoned by its crew in the Kassel area, April 1945. The vehicle represents the experimental type of the *octopus* camouflage scheme applied on *Königstiger* tanks in the last weeks of World War II. [Kagero Archive]

Panzerkampfwagen VI Ausf. B with *Henschel* turret (tactical number: 233) of the 2nd Company of *schwere Panzer Abteilung 503*. Budapest, October 1944. [Bundesarchiv]

the Second World War. It was characterized by a barrel with an overall length of 6595 mm and the weight of 2,3 t. At the end of the tube a massive, two-chamber muzzle brake was installed. The whole set was also equipped with pneumatic-hydraulic recoil mechanism (the barrel moved back by an average of 480 mm after each shot).

There was a stowage of 72 88-milimeter cartridges transported at one time inside the vehicle, but it happened that at the expense of comfort service and, above all, the safety crew decided to increase this number up to 8 pieces more. Nine variants of ammunition was dedicated to *8,8 cm KwK 43 L/71* cannon. The most effective, armor-piercing *Panzergranate 40/43* which muzzle velocity reached 1100 m/s was able to penetrate at the distance of 2 km, the 153 mm thick armor plate (at the distance of 500 meters - more than 200 mm thick one).

There was the monocular *Turmzielfernrohr 9d/1* viewfinder with the magnification from three to six times installed in the majority of *Royal Tigers* (and the binocular *TZF 9b* in case of first production series tanks and prototypes). There were separate scales provided for each type of ammunition: in the case of anti-tank projectiles measurements were performed using a scale in red, kinetic energy penetrator or long-rod penetrator ones – in green, high explosive anti-tank warhead ones – in yellow and high explosive – in black.

Tabele 4. *Pz.Kpfw. VI Ausf. B* heavy tank armor		
	Thickness	Slope
Chassis – front	150 mm	50°
Chassis – sides	80 mm	25°
Chassis – rear	80 mm	30°
Chassis - top	40 mm	90°
Chassis – bottom	25 mm	90°
Turret (Porsche Model) – front	110 mm	rounded
Turret (Porsche Model) – sides	80 mm	30°
Turret (Porsche Model) – turret	40 mm	77°–90°
Turret (Henschel Model) – front	180 mm	9°
Turret (Henschel Model) – sides	80 mm	21°
Turret (Henschel Model) – top	40 mm	78°–90°
Turret (Henschel Model) – gun mantlet	100 mm	–

The *Königstiger* additional weapon was a pair of 7.92 mm Maschinengewehr 34 machine guns (the tank version). One of them was installed in the spherical, identical to that installed in *Pz.Kpfw. V Panther* medium tank cupola, to the right of the front armor plate, the second, featuring *KgZF 2* viewfinder, on the right side of the turret front plate. The machine gun ammunition was 5850 blocked in 150 pieces magazines. Apart of thet, the crew of five had at its disposal personal weapons: 9 mm and 7.65 mm pistols and, transported inside the vehicle, *9 mm Maschinenpistole 40* machine pistols.

The communication between vehicles in a platoon enabled the *Funkgerätsatz 5 type C* (27-33 MHz) radio transmitter and the *Fu 2e* receiver with 2000 mm length *Stabantenne* antenna rod mounted in the hard-rubber socket on the turret. The effective range of the voice communication was 13 km and 16 km using the Morsea alphabet. *Panzerbefehlswagen VI Ausf. B* command vehicles, as it was mentioned earlier, could have lead broadcasting from more than four times longer distance – circa about 80 km by the key.

The new German heavy tank belonged to the largest mass-produced, tracked combat vehicles of the World War Two. Its length was 10300 mm, width: 37,600 mm and height 3080 mm. In the variant with *Henschel Model* turret its weight exceeded 68 t, of which 28 t weighed the hull itself (the turret: 13.5 t). Exemplars equipped version of the *Porsche Model* turret were about 500 kg lighter.

Combat use theory

According to the *Panzerwaffe* current theory at the time of putting *King Tigers* into service there were intended to form the spearhead of independent heavy tank battalions of German land forces (*schwere Heeres Panzer Abteilung*) and the *Waffen-SS* (*schwere SS Panzer Abteilung*).

As far as *Kriegsstärknachweisung 1107b (freie Gliederung)* of June 1, 1944 were concerned, each of German heavy independent tank battalions was to consist of forty-five machines. Three of them, mostly the *Panzerbefehlswagen* ones, were deployed to the commanding subunit (*Stabskompanie*) – the battalion headquarters. The remaining forty two, in the groups of fourteen were separated into each of the three tank companies (*Kompanie*). Each company (*Zug*) consisted of three platoons with four tanks and the company headquarters (*Zug Führung*) This organization formula was confirmed by *Kriegsstärknachweisung 1107d (freie Gliederung)* of November 1, 1944 and its presented by the Diagram 1.

In fact, the allocation was dependent on the current production and repairs conducted by field workshops. Majority of *Königstiger* exemplars – 247, were sent to units operating on the Eastern Front. 194 replenished forces in the West, and

Panzerkampfwagen VI Ausf. B with *Henschel* turret (tactical number: 231) belonging to the 2nd Company of *schwere Panzer Abteilung* 503. Budapest, October 1944. [Bundesarchiv]

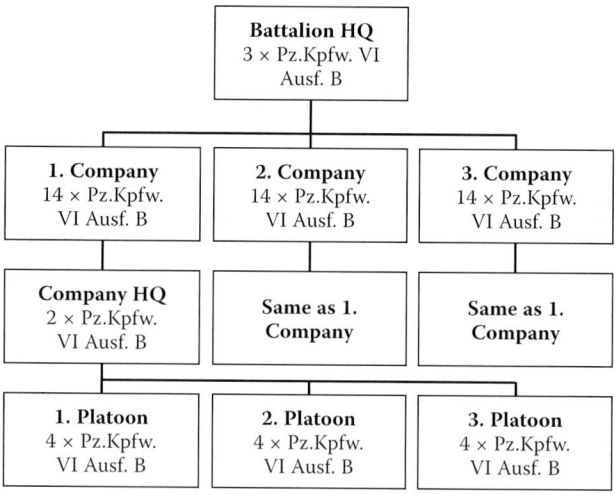

Diagram 1: *Pz.Kpfw. VI Ausf. B* deployment in the *Heer* and *Waffen-SS* independent heavy tank battalion *(schwere Panzer Abteilung)* according to *KStN 1107b (fG)* and *KStN 1107d (fG)*

Total amount: 45 Pz.Kpfw. VI Ausf. B heavy tanks in battalion and 14 ones in company.

One of *Panzerkampfwagen VI Ausf. B* with *Henschel* turret belonging to *schwere Panzer Abteilung 503* photographed in Budapest, October 1944. The tactical number 200 indicates that was the 2nd Company commander tank. [Bundesarchiv]

28 detained in reserve (including 13 in the composition of the Reserve Army – *Ersatzheer*). It should be noted that not all vehicles were deployed in independent tank battalions. Six *Royal Tigers* (with the *Porsche Model* turret) were subordinated to *Funklenk Panzer Kompanie 316* being, theoretically, an element of *Panzer Lehr Division*. A few pieces, in March 1945 bolster also the *Feldhernhalle* Armored Division stationed in Austria.

In line with the tactical regulations, the new heavy tanks proved themselves most effectively during the fighting at long range, without being exposed to destruction by the enemy fire. In that case they could effectively eliminate all of armored vehicles of the anti-allied forces on each of the European theaters of operations. In the case of shorter distances an essential rule were the protection of the *Royal Tigers* by *Panzergrenadiers* or other, more mobile vehicles, for instance *Sturmgeschütz* or properly armed *Sd.Kfz. 251* half-tracks.

King Tigers in combat

Panzerkampfwagen VI Ausf. B debuted on the fronts of World War II in the early summer of 1944. Soldiers of the allied coalition met them both on stretched from the southern shore of the Baltic Sea to the Balkans the eastern front, as well as in France, Belgium and West Germany. Episodes below were selected from the history of a few German independent heavy tank battalions, in which *Königstiger* tanks played an significant role. Some of them, what is important from the point of view of the author, occurred on the territory of present-day Poland.

Dressed in typical black uniforms of the German tankers crew members of *Panzerkampfwagen VI Ausf. B* with *Henschel* turret (tactical number: 233) of *schwere Panzer Abteilung 503* photographed in Autumn 1944. Note the 180 mm thick front armor plate of the *Königstiger* tank and the *Zimmerit* antimagnetic coat applied on the turret. [Bundesarchiv]

Panzerkampfwagen VI Ausf. B with *Henschel* turret (tactical number: 231) belonging to the 2nd Company of *schwere Panzer Abteilung 503*. Budapest, October 1944. [Bundesarchiv]

Difficult premiere in Normandy

There was three German heavy tank battalions sent to fight against Anglo-American forces during the Normandy campaign. Two of them: *schwere SS Panzer Abteilung 101* and *schwere SS Panzer Abteilung 102* represented the infamous *Waffen-SS*, another one – *schwere Heeres Panzer Abteilung 503* belonged to the III Reich, *Wehrmacht* land forces. That time, from that three independent units, the Royal Tigers appeared only in the last one. The others were armed with *Panzerkampfwagen VI Tiger Ausführung E/H1* tracked vehicles, better known as *Tiger Is*.

The 503rd independent heavy tank battalion was created in Neuruppin, in April 1942. Originally it was planned to direct the unit to North Africa, where he had to support military operations of the famous *Desert Fox* – Erwin Rommel forces, however, due to the critical situation on the eastern front, it went to the Soviet Union. The battle debut of *schwere Heeres Panzer Abteilung 503*, armed with *Tiger I* tanks took place on January 5, 1943 in the vicinity of Stavropol. In the following months, presented battalion took part in the battles at Kursk and Belgorod. At the beginning of 1944 its soldiers fastened the defence lines at Uman and Cherkassy pocket, and later, in the Tarnopol and Kaments Podolski area. In late spring the 503rd was withdrawn to Ohrdurf in Thuringia, Germany.

At the end of May 1944 the unit, at that time commanded by *Hauptmann* Rolf Fromme was incorporated into Panzer Group West (*Panzergruppe West*). Although launched June 6 Allied invasion of Normandy, the battalion was decided to leave in the reserve. Ten days later twelve *Pz.Kpfw. VI Ausf. B* with *Porsche Model* turrets reached the place of its deployment. Along with a pair of *Pz.Kpfw. VI Ausf. E* all of them were assigned to the 1st Company, which commander was *Hauptmann* Walter Scherf.

June 27, 1944 r. *schwere Heeres Panzer Abteilung 503* rolled from Germany to France reaching, July 2, Dreux. Another 200 km to the first line, tanks moved using roads, generally at night. Gathered in the village Ruppieres near Caen, five days later, the crew reported combat readiness. All vehicles of the battalion were subordinated to the staff of the German 22nd Armored Regiment of *21. Panzer Division*.

The first battle with *Royal Tigers* in the first line took place on July 11. Opponent of the Germans proved to be the British, armed with United States made *M4 Sherman* medium tanks. Their 75-mm guns firing even at 200 m distance, were not able to successfully harm powerfully armored *Pz.Kpfw. VI Ausf. B* of *Hauptmann* Scherf Company. After this episode, the unit went to Emieville. They found the outbreak of Operation *Goodwood* there.

July 18, 1944 r. in the Le Prieuré area, *Königstiger* tanks attacked the positions occupied by the British 23rd Hussars and the Coldstream Guards, this time, not without losses. Maneuvering through full of bomb craters field, the vehicles with tactical numbers 100 and 101 were stopped by the artillery and tank fire and then, abandoned by their crews. Another one, (tactical number 111) was eliminated by the direct hit from the 17-pounder gun of *Sherman Firefly*.

Nearly at the same time one of the most extraordinary events with the present type of vehicle took place. In the evening, near Cagny, the *King Tiger* (tactical number 122 belonging to the 2nd Platoon of the 1st Company) crew lost during the day-long fights, had been surprised by the pair of *Shermans* of the *Irish Guards*. Armed in the 75-mm gun *M4* tank nicknamed *Ballyragget*, commanded by Lieutenant John Reginald Gorman, rammed the German colossus to the surprise of both sides, eliminating it from further fighting.

In subsequent days, Walter Scherf's unit tanks supported the grenadiers of *1. SS Panzer Division Leibstandarte Adolf Hitler* during the fighting in the Bourgebous Ridge. July 29 the *schwere Heeres Panzer Abteilung 503* 1st Company was withdrawn to Mailly-le-Camp near Troyes, where it was reinforced with another, brand-new *Porsche*-turreted *King Tigers*. Another group of this vehicles were subordinated to the 3rd Company at the end of July. That unit, in the course of railroad dislocation, somewhere between Sezanne and Esterney became the target of an allied aircraft attack. The *P-47* planes managed to destroy one heavy tank. Others, because of its weight could not have reached any appropriate crossing over the Seine. According to that fact, they did not get at Normandy. Later they were used in the fights near Amiens. September 22, 1944 r., after the defeat of the German army at Falaise, *Hauptmann* Fromme's subordinates were sent to the Sennelager proving grounds near Paderborn, and there received *Pz.Kpfw. VI Ausf. B* tanks with *Henschel Model* turrets. Few weeks later the 503rd battalion were on its way to Hungary.

Another armed with Königstiger Panzerwaffe unit sent to Normandy was *Funklenk Panzer Kompanie 316*. It was created

Panzerkampfwagen VI Ausf. B with Porsche Model turret tanks of the 1st Company of schwere Panzer Abteilung 503 during the combat training near Ohrdurf, June 1944. In the same month this unit was deployed to Normandy to fight against the allied invasion. [Bundesarchiv]

in April 1943 in Eisenach, from where it has been transferred to Fallingbostel. There, February 18, 1944, the crews received a half-dozen of new German heavy tanks with a *Porsche Model* turrets. The whole company, only in theory, were incorporated to the 130th Armored Regiment of *Panzer-Lehr Division*.

Shortly after the Allied landing on the southern shore of the English Channel, the presented unit were sent to Châteaudun in the Orleans area. What happened next is the subject of dispute between military historians even today. Although nearly 70-ton giants most likely had not had established any combat contact with the enemy, the crews decided to abandon their vehicles and, arbitrarily, leave the assigned defensive positions. Theme of their conduct remains unknown. It has been suggested that the impact on this attitude was lack of konwlege how to effectively use the new weapon, rumors of their only experimental or propaganda use, and above all (and this seems the most likely) a high failure rate, resulting in the permanent immobilizing of *Royal Tigers*.

All heavy tanks of *Funklenk Panzer Kompanie 316* were left between 16 and 20 June 1944. Exact date of abandonment by the crew of each vehicle marked with 02, 03, 10, 11, 12 and 13 tactical numbers as well as place of leaving are presented in Table 3. In the same month, all of *Königtigers* were seized by the *US Army*. At the French fields the armored giants remained until the early fifties.

The 316th Company itself, July 2, 1944 was withdrawn to Reims, where it was transformed in the 1st Company of *Funklenk-Panzer Abteilung 302*. Equipped with *Sturmgeschütz III Ausf. G* assault guns and *schwere Ladungsträger Borgward B IV* tracked explosives carriers, was transferred to Poland. It was used, among others, during the suppression of the Warsaw Uprising in August and September 1944.

Table 5. Abandoning of *Pz.Kpfw. VI Ausf. B* heavy tanks subordinated to *Funklenk Panzer Kompanie 316*, June 1944.

Tactical number	Date of abandoning	Place of abandoning
02	probably 19.06.1944 r.	Janville
03	probably 16.06.1944 r.	Nogent-Le-Routrou
10	18.06.1944 r.	Varize
11	17.06.1944 r.	Châteaudun
12	17.06.1944 r.	Châteaudun
13	17.06.1944 r.	Châteaudun

The Staszów hecatomb

In July 1944, in Ohrdurf in Thuringia (Germany), decimated during the battles in Tunisia, and then: Berezina, 501 independent battalion of heavy tanks (*schwere Heeres Panzer Abteilung 501*) had been reconstucted. Its theater of operations, once again, had become the eastern front. In this part of Europe, after successfully launching the *Bagration* Operation of the Red Army, majority of Army Group North Ukraine units were in desperate need of support. One of the endangered areas were, being the main target of the Soviet 6th Guards Armoured Corps region of Kielce. This unit, being the first opponent of *Pz.Kpfw. VI Ausf. B* crews in the east, after the he struggles in the early days of *Bagration* had altogether only thirty-nine tanks. Among them, in theory, only eleven *IS-2*s could be a real threat to the new German heavy tanks.

Commanded by *Major* von Legat battalion reached the Jedreczewo railway station on August 5, 1944. After that the *Royal*

Tigers moved to the Sandomierz bridgehead. There were ten tanks which were lost during this march because of mechanical failures. He also appeared The problem of load capacity of bridges also appeared, in most cases, weighing 68 t vehicles were not able to cross without additional support by combat engineers. Only eight *Königstiger* were ready for action on August 11. Other were sent to being repaired by field workshops.

The next day the 501st battalion were ordered to support the *16. Panzer Division*, attacking from the Chmeilnik area, Staszów. Due to the disregard of the enemy and the lack of proper reconnaissance, near the village of Ogłędów, German tanks, without changing the narrower transport tracks to 800 mm wide combat ones, towing in sandy soil entered straight into the barrel of well-camouflaged guns and tanks of the Red Army. Without protection of infantry and lighter combat vehicles, *King Tigers* become an easy target for the Soviets. At first, shots from 85 and 122 mm tank cannons eliminated two of German colossus. Direct hits of Porsche Model turrets, next to the interior ammunition racks caused huge explosions. The third *Pz.Kpfw. VI Ausf. B*, after its track had been brought, were destroyed by an artillery fire.

August 13 the battle raged once again. Like the day before, it ended in the victory of the Red Army. Three *Pz.Kpfw. VI Ausf. B* with *Henschel Model* turrets bering tactical numbers 002, 502 and 234, only slightly damaged felt in the Soviet hands. The first two were transported to Kubinka near Moscow. Number 002 was tested on the proving grounds, among others, with intense fire from Red Army tank guns and anti-tank guns, and the number 502, representing a command variant, until today could be seen you can enjoy in armored weapon museum there. Its worth to be said, that the 234 *King Tiger*, after trying to transport it behind the frontline by the Soviets, finally were abandoned.

In general, during the Staszów-Ogłędów battle a dozen of *Königstiger* tanks of *schwere Heeres Panzer Abteilung 501* had been lost. Similar to the premiere in the West, it was caused because of the lack of knowledge of the tactical rules of using the new *Panzerwaffe* weapon, as well as its technical weaknesses, especially an excessive burden of *Maybach* engine and appearing very often transmission failures. That all led to permanent tank immobilization and as a result, leaving in in the battlefield.

After the defeat in the Sandomierz bridgehead, 501st independent heavy tank battalion was transferred to the Pilica River area. Its commander, *Major* von Legat, accused of collaborating with the fraction, which on July 20, 1944, conducted a failed attempt on the life of Adolf Hitler, lost his position. At the beginning of 1945, the unit took part in attempts to stop the Soviet offensive, which started from the Vistula to the Oder.

The *Königstiger* combat debut on the Eastern Front, looked forward to the legend. Present days, many residents of Staszów area, in particular the village of Bogoria, in the neighboring

Panzerkampfwagen VI Ausf. B with *Porsche* turret tanks of the 1st Company of *schwere Panzer Abteilung 503*, Château de Canteloup area, July 1944. [Bundesarchiv]

Panzerkampfwagen VI Ausf. B with *Porsche* turret tanks of the 1st Company of *schwere Panzer Abteilung 503*, Château de Canteloup area, July 1944. [Bundesarchiv]

forest which still can be seen trenchers and other traces of the battles of 1944, suggest that at night there were all calibers weapon fires heard in the forest. Ghosts in German uniforms could also be seen there, as well as unburied bodies of the dead more than seventy years ago. There are probably soldiers of 501st battalion who were not managed to escape the Soviet vengeance among.

Royal Tigers in Ardennes

Panzerkampfwagen VI Ausf. B tanks drifting through the snowy forests of the Ardennes are one of the most classic images that are associated with the actually described *Panzerwaffe* vehicle. There were more than forty such vehicles used during the German 1944/1945 counter-offensive in the French-Belgium border area. Next to them on the front moved twenty-one *Jagdpanzer VI Jagdtiger* tank destroyer, being used only as an experimental weapon.

Thirty *Royal Tigers*, including eleven transferred from *schwere Heeres Panzer Abteilung 509*, at the end of November reached three companies of the 501st SS heavy tank battalion (*schwere SS Panzer Abteilung 501*), commanded by *SS-Obersturmbannführer* Heinz von Westernhagen. This unit was incorporated into Combat Group *Peiper* (*Kampfgruppe Peiper*) with *SS-Obersturmbannführer* Joachim Peiper, who was leading 1st SS Panzer Regiment, as a commander. This unit, being a part of *1. SS Panzer Division Leibstandarte Adolf Hitler* was believed to be the elite of the armed forces of the Third Reich. On the eve of offensive codenamed *Herbstnebel* (*Autumn Mist*), the battalion had fifteen machines in combat readiness (twenty according to Jean Paul Pallud). Other were being repaired, or on their ways from depots and factories in Germany.

SS-Obersturmbannführer von Westernhagen's heavy tanks started operation in the Losheim area, on Saturday, December 16, 1944 around 10.00 am. Along with all Joachim Peiper's unit they moved *Rollbahn D* route, toward Stavelot, La Gleize, Stoumont and St. Séverin, intending within a few hours to reach the shore of the Meuse south of Clermont. There was Combat Gropu Sandig (Kampfgruppe Sandig) built on the basis of the *SS Panzergrenadier Regiment 2* running just behind the armored columns. Breaking through the columns of German vehicles blocked the road at the end of the first day of operation the 501st SS battalion reached Lanzerath.

According to preserved nowadays archival material, *Pz.Kpfw. VI Ausf. B* belonging to *Kampfgruppe Peiper* during the first days of action in the Ardennes appeared, among others, in Tondorf and, December 18, Ligneuville. In the latter, on the personal wishes of Combat Group commander, there was one of Fallschirmjäger Regiment 9 of the German 3rd Airborne Division transferred in the ranks of the SS unit and use as *Königstiger* riders and, in case of being attacked by the enemy infantry, its close-combat defenders. On the same day, one of the 68-ton giants was lost in Stavelot. The vehicle bearing tactical number 105 and belonging to the commander of the 1st Company of *schwere SS Panzer Abteilung 501*, *SS-Obersturmführer* Jürgen Wessel stuck on Rue St. Emilon, and was abandoned there.

The next day the *King Tigers* spearhead reached La Gleize. All of tanks were immobilized there because lack of fuel. At least seven *Pz.Kpfw. VI Ausf. B*s were lost in the town area. Every of them have been abandoned by the crew after firing the entire stock of main armament ammunition. Other vehicles, using, inter alia, the fuel seized from destroyed *US Army* columns, moved to the area of Bastogne, providing fire support during its siege.

As in one of his books points Steven Zaloga, the last *Königstiger* in the Ardennes was set on fire by its crew on December 25, 1944 near Ambleve. It was Panzerbefehlswagen VI Ausf. B (tactical number 008) of the command section of the 501st SS battalion. Previously, the tank stopped because of lack of fuel and mechanical failure. The German used it as an artillery bunker armed with powerful 88-milimeters gun.

In the struggle for Pomerania

Another unit of *Panzerwaffe* armed with *Royal Tigers*, which fought on the territory of present-day Poland is the 503rd SS heavy tank battalion (*schwere SS Panzer Abteilung 503*). The genesis of this unit, at the beginning of 1945 commanded by *SS-Sturmbannführer* Fritz Herzig, was set up in 1943 and the 8th Company of *3. SS Panzergrenadier Division* (later: *3. SS Panzer Division*) *Totenkopf* which *Pz.Kpfw. VI Ausf. E* tanks,

Panzerkampfwagen VI Ausf. B with *Henschel* turret tanks of *schwere Panzer Abteilung 503* during its presentation in Sennelager, September 1944. This version of *Königstiger* were to substitute vehicles lost by the unit during the Normandy campaign. [Bundesarchiv]

inter alia, took part in the battle of Kursk. At the end of the penultimate year of the Second World War, soldiers of the 503rd SS battalion received thirty nine of previously planned forty five *Panzerkampfwagen VI Ausf. B* tracked giants.

January 25, 1945 r. presented formation was sent over the Oder River as a support of III SS Panzer Korps, defending its positions in the western part of Pomerania. The heavy tanks had been earlier divided into two groups. The first one, composed of twelve machines including the batttalion's commander vehicle moved to Recz (in 1945: Reetz), another, to transformed into a fortress Kostrzyn nad Odrą (Küstrin). The railway platforms with *Königstiger*s arrived at the train station the first of the above-mentioned towns three days later. There, the crews were ordered to move to the line of Kalisz Pomorski (Kallies)-Drawno (Drawehn). January 31, near the village of Radęcin (Regenthin) *SS-Sturmbannführer* Herzig's battalion lost one of its tanks (as it was established by members of Polish Stowarzyszenie Archeologii Militarnej Pomorze, the vehicle still stood on the battlefield a few years after the war). Others set off to Choszczna (Arnswalde).

SS *Royal Tigers* clashed with Soviet armored spearhed once again on February 3 and 4, in the south of the city, in the area of Zamęcin (Sammenthin) and Gleźno (Hohenwald). Finally, all eleven *Pz.Kpfw. VI Ausf. B* drove to Choszczno. Among them was the vehicle of the future *schwere SS Panzer Abteilung 503* ace, *SS-Untersturmführer* Karl Bromann that after damage of control mechanism was towed to the vicinity Choszczno church. February 6, the town was encircled by the Red Army. Ultimately, operating within nine days later launched Operation *Sonnenwende* (Solstice) – the German counter-offensive in the region of Stargard Szczeciński (Stargard in Pommern), 68-ton colossuses involved in breaking out, to enable the withdrawal the significant number of Arnswalde civilian inhabitants. Earlier,

on February 9, near the village of Suliborek (Klein Silber), there were three *Königstiger* left on the battlefield.

Similar to Staszów-Oględów battle, the legend accreted also around Choszczno armored clash. According to some local enthusiasts, there is at least one German tank sunk in the Klukom Lake situated in the city center. It is hard to establish whether the vehicle belonged to *SS-Sturmbannführer* Herzig's unit or any other representing the Third Reich forces. It is told, that the vehicle sank during the passage through the frozen lake. Its research was without a success carried out in 2011.

On the night of 17 to 18 February 1945 the 503rd SS heavy tank battalion was again in rail transport. *Royal Tigers* used almost as armored artillery wagons, moved toward the Gulf of Gdansk firing their guns at Soviet positions in the area of Tczew, Pruszcz Gdański and Gdańsk-Wrzeszcz. For their brothers in arms there was one crew which members quickly became the unit heroes. It was led by aforementioned *SS-Untersturmführer* Bromann. During the February and March combat, it managed to destroy sixty six tanks and self-propelled guns of the enemy (including vehicles of the Polish 1st Armoured Brigade Bohaterów Westerplatte), forty four towed guns and fifteen cars. The crew achievements were recorded even in the official army high command report given on April 10, 1945. It was Karl Bromann himself, who was seriously wounded in the head and hands during the battle of Gdańsk and Gdynia. A little later, hit by shrapnel he lost his eye. March 27, *SS-Untersturmführer* Bromann was taken to the hospital and by Hel and Świnoujście (Swinemünde) evacuated to Germany. April 29 he was awarded the Knight's Cross of the Iron Cross.

While part of *schwere SS Panzer Abteilung 503* presented above was pouring blood on the Baltic coast, another one supported the Festung Kűstron garrison during the heavy fighting in the Odra river basin. There had been not more than six tanks operative after that battle. All of them were deployed to *11. SS Panzer Grenadier Division Nordland*, defending Berlin. The last destroyed in World War Two *King Tiger* belonged strictly to this unit. It was hit by the Soviet tank or artillery fire in the night of May 2, 1945 in Spandau.

There was another 503rd SS battalion *Königstiger* ace appearing during the Red Army siege of Berlin. It was *SS-Hauptscharführer* Karl Körner, commander of one of the 2nd Company platoons. In the last days of April 1945, his vehicle took part in the German grenadiers counter-attack near Bollersdorf. Leading the spearhead, the crew found itself face to face with two *IS-2* heavy tanks. One of them was destroyed by direct hit of 8.8 cm KwK 43 L/71 gun, the second, abandoned in the anti-tank ditch trying to withdraw. Karl Körner moved on. A few moments later, he was able to surprise the column of eleven *IS-2*s during refueling and replenishing main armament and machine guns ammunition. In a few minutes they were destroyed too. Before the Germans finally cut their offensive, the crew was able to eliminate another thirty nine other enemy vehicles. Finally, on April 29, 1945 when *SS-Hauptscharführer* Körner was receiving the Knight's Cross of the Iron Cross in the bunker under the Reich Chancellery, the account of his crew was more than one hundred Soviet combat vehicles. In the day of capitulation of Berlin, they were fighting in Charlottenburg.

Summary

Without a doubt *Panzerkampfwagen VI Tiger Ausf. B* should be counted among the most efficient tracked combat vehicles, which were used on all fronts of World War II. Armed with a powerful 88-millimeter main gun, wreaked havoc in the ranks of the Allied soldiers, though, as show, among others, episodes presented in this book, certainly it was not the vehicle impossible to destroy. Weaknesses of the *Royal Tiger* was definitely a technical imperfections, the same that summer of 1943, eliminated *Pz.Kpfw. VI Ausf. E* and *Pz.Kpfw V Ausf. D* tanks during its premiere at Kursk. These problems, including those stemming from the overload of the 700 HP *Maybach* engine or transmission, could not be definitively eliminated until the World War Two ended. Whatever, not exceeding five hundred exemplars of *Königstiger* manufactured in Kassel, was not able to change the dire state of the Third Reich in the final period of the last global conflict.

Today the 68-ton giants from the *Henschel udn Sohn* factory are preserved in several European museums. It could be found in the French *Musee des Blindes* in Saumur, *Schweizerisches Militärmuseum* in Full (Switzerland), *Munster Panzer Museum* in Germany and armored weapon museum in Kubinka near Moscow, where the command tank destroyed during the Staszów-Oględów battle is exhibited. There are two *Royal Tigers* present in the United Kingdom: the first in the Royal Armoured Corps Tank Museum Bovington, another, Military Royal College of Science Shrivenham. *Pz.Kpfw. VI Ausf. B* also complements the National Armor and Cavalry Museum in Fort Benning (USA) collection.

Another one in form of a monument could be seen in front of December 44 Museum in La Gleize, Belgium. Belonging to *Kampfgruppe Peiper* vehicle was lost by its *schwere SS Panzer Abteilung 501* crew in the second half of December 1944, in the nearby Wérimont Farm.

Tabele 6. *Pz.Kpfw. VI Ausf. B* heavy tank technical data	
Measurments	-
Length	10300 mm
Width	3760 mm
Heighth	3080 mm
Combat weight	68 t
Armor	25 – 180 mm
Engine power	700 HP
Fuel capacity	830 l
Fuel road consumption	650 l/100 km
Maximum speed	35 km/h
Armament	-
Main	8.8 cm KWK 43 L/71
Support	2 x 7,92 mm MG34
Ammunition capacity	-
Main gun	72
Machine guns	5850
Radio set	FuG 5
Crew	5

Wehrmacht tank crew member applying the camouflage scheme on one of the *Panzerkampfwagen VI Ausf. B* with *Henschel* turret tanks of *schwere Panzer Abteilung 503*, 1944. [Bundesarchiv]

Sheet 1
© Drawings by Mariusz Suliga

Tiger II Ausf. B with Henschel turret (September 1944).

1:35

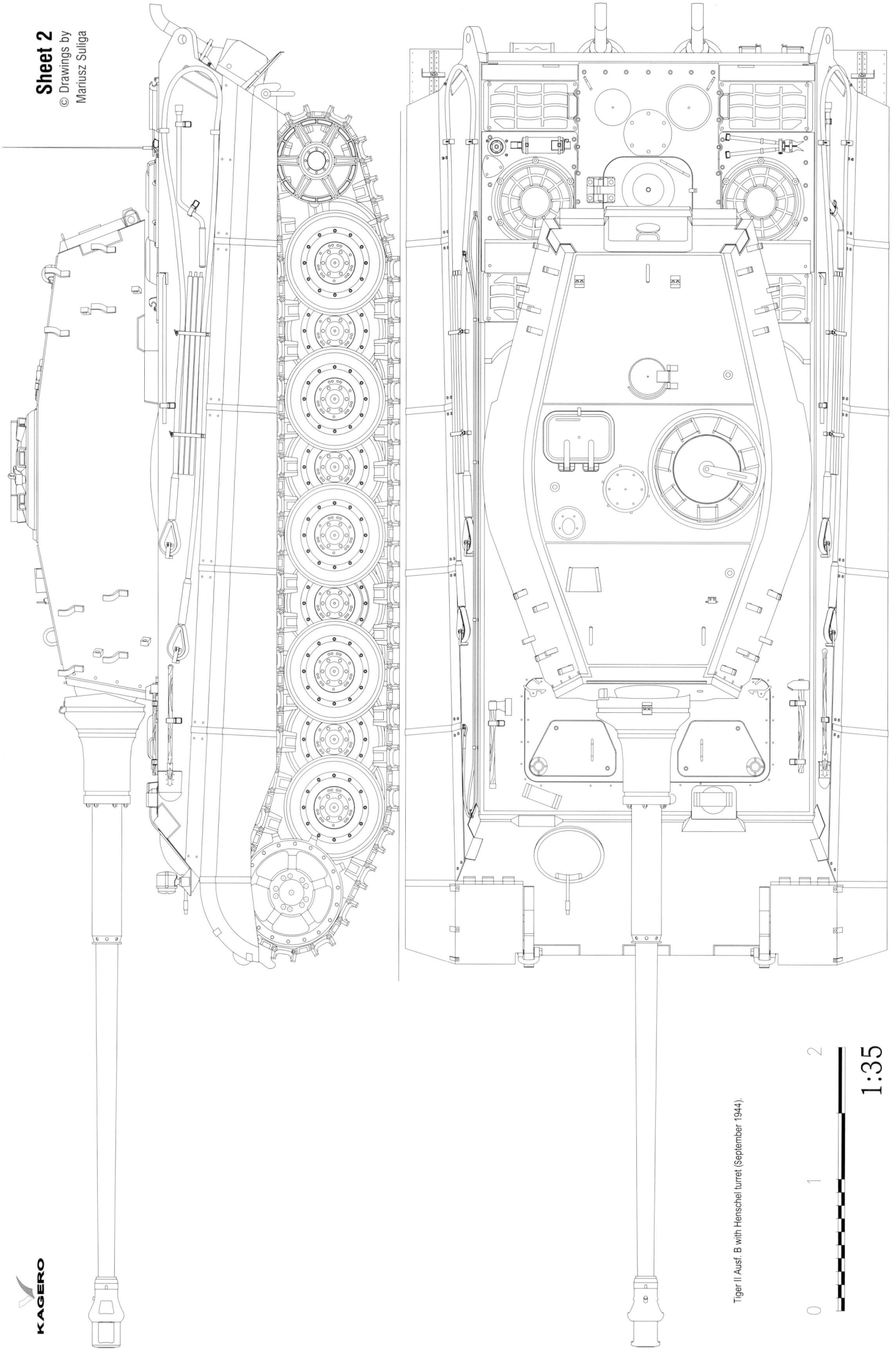

Tiger II Ausf. B with Henschel turret (September 1944).

Sheet 3

© Drawings by Mariusz Suliga

Tiger II Ausf. B with Porsche turret (June 1944).

1:35

KAGERO

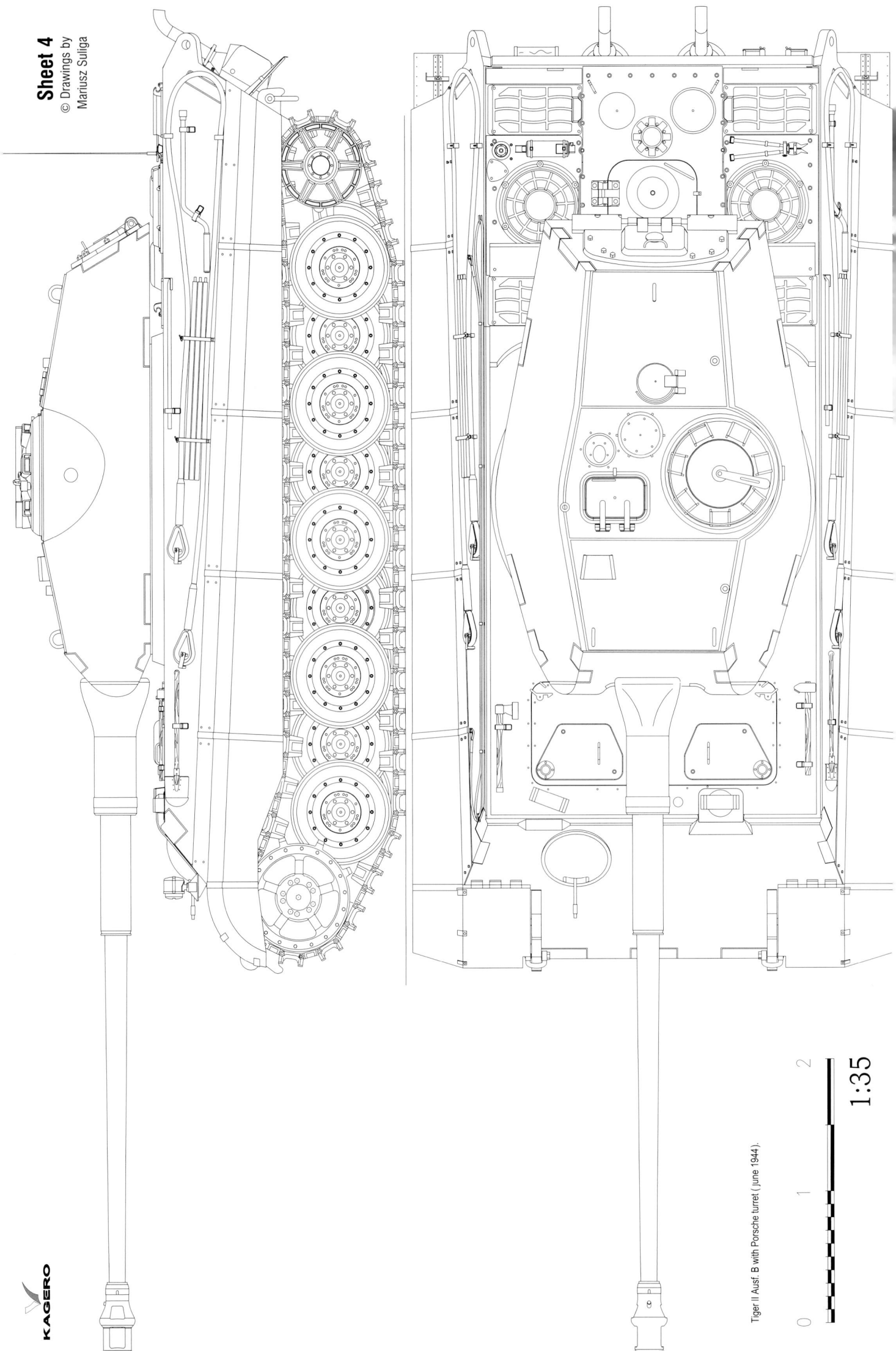

Tiger II Ausf. B with Porsche turret (june 1944).

1:35

Sheet 5

© Drawings by
Mariusz Suliga

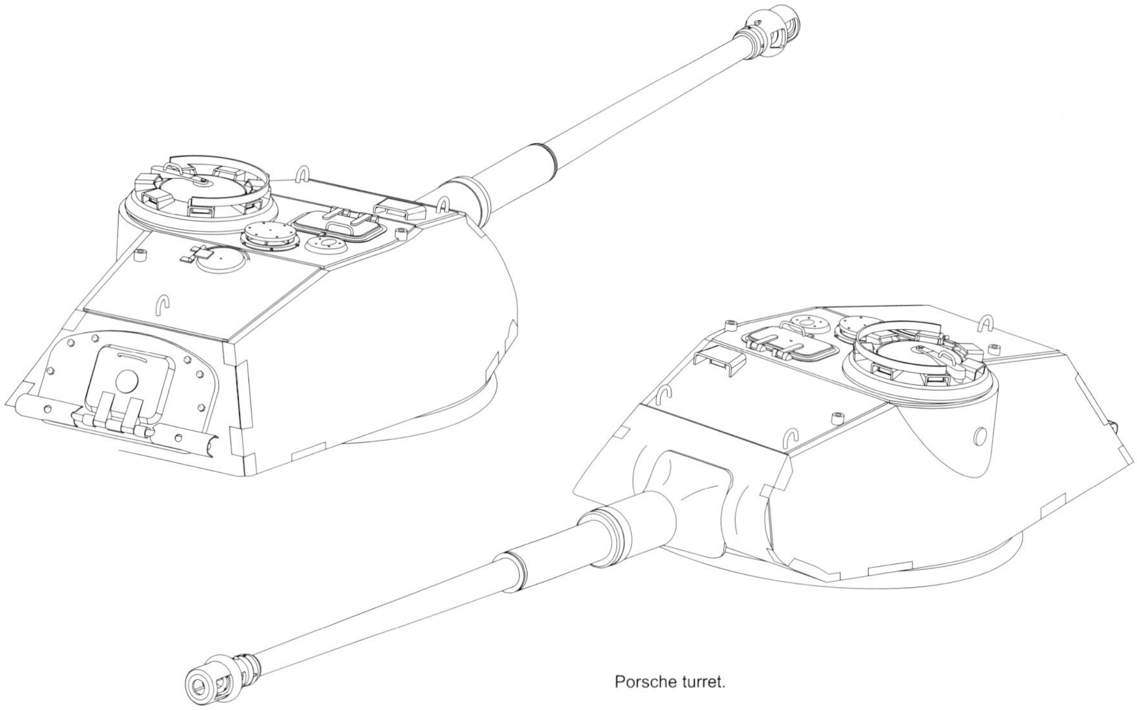

Porsche turret.

Henschel turret.

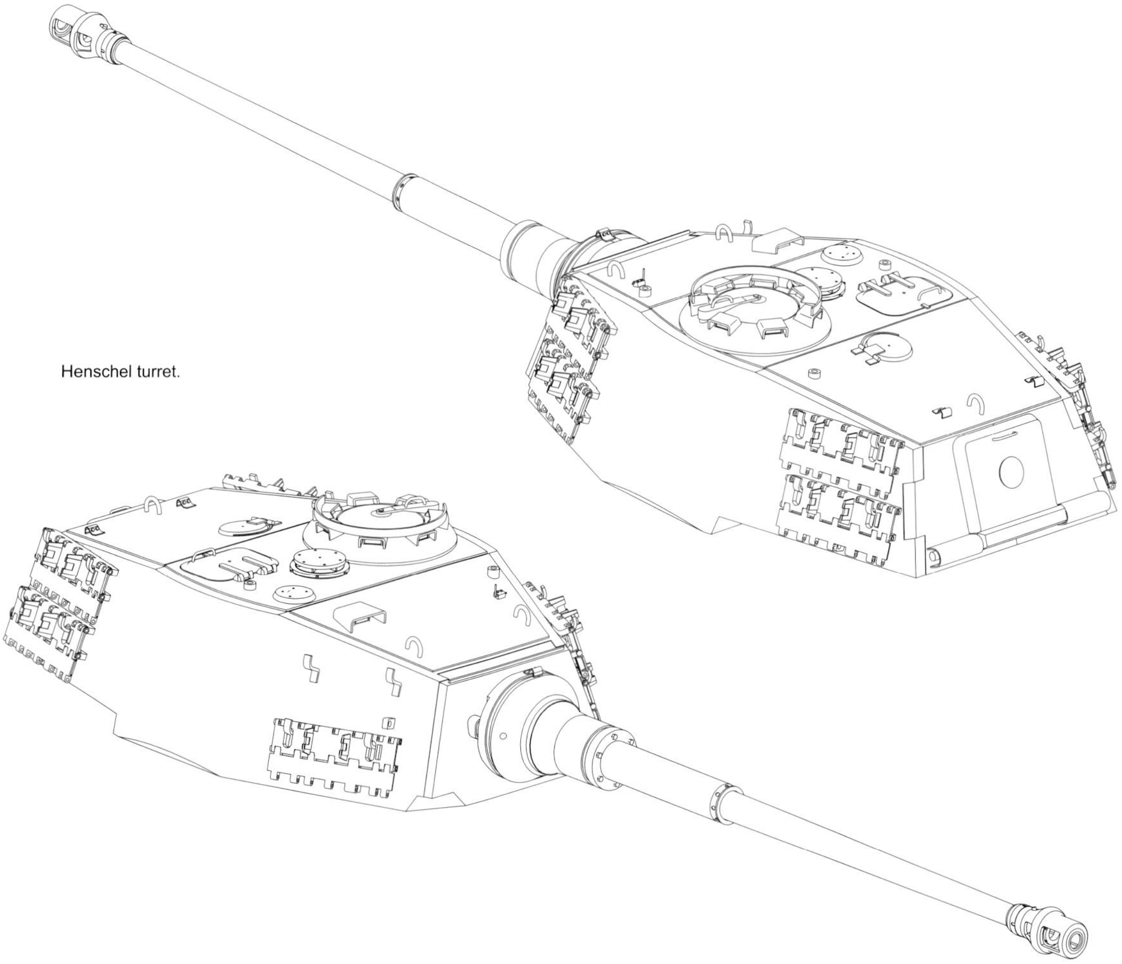

Sheet 12

© Drawings by
Mariusz Suliga

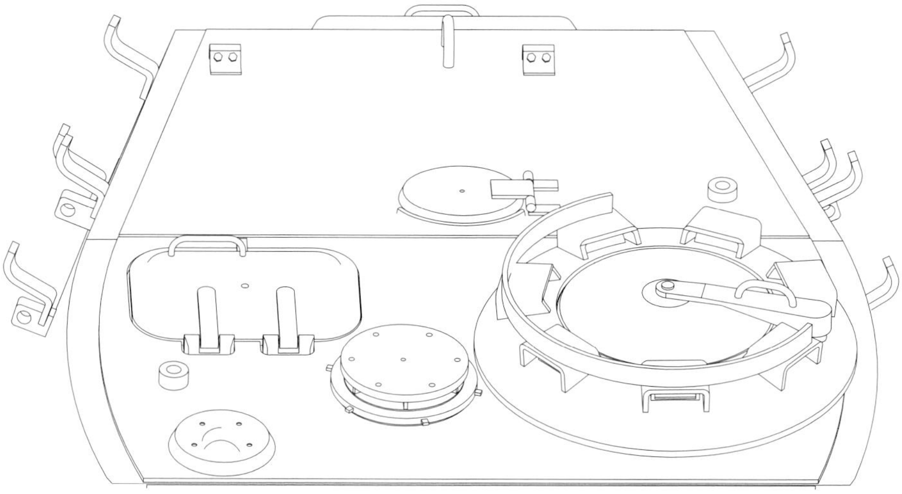

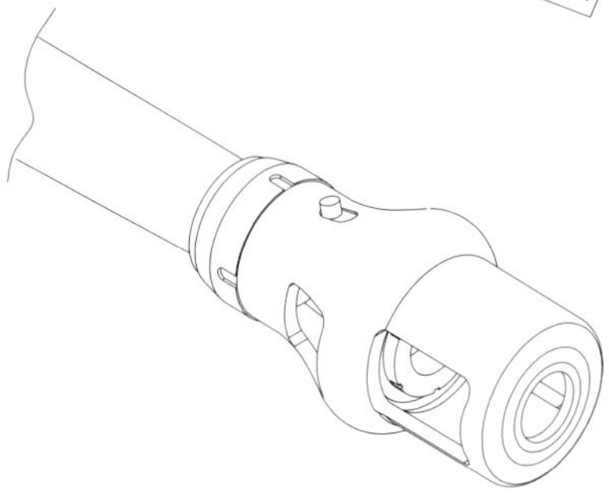

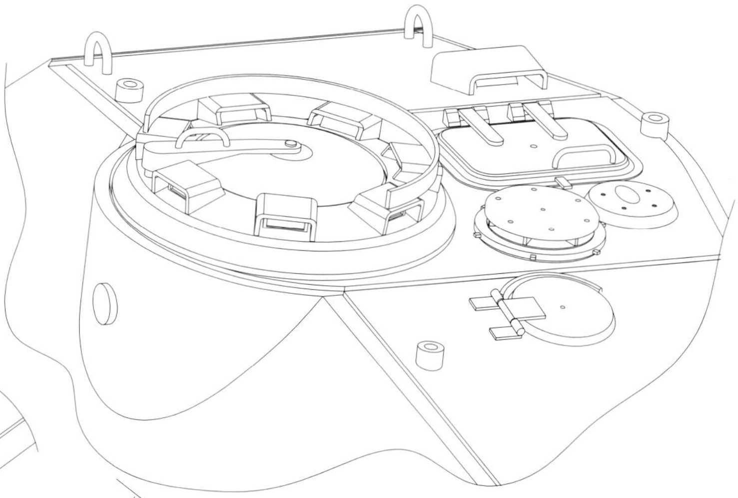

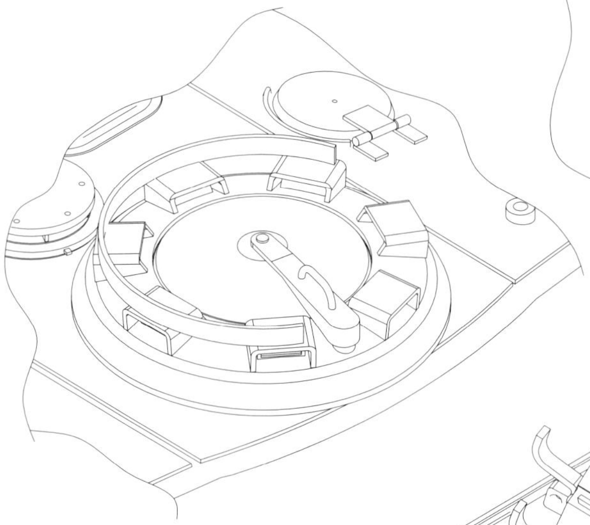

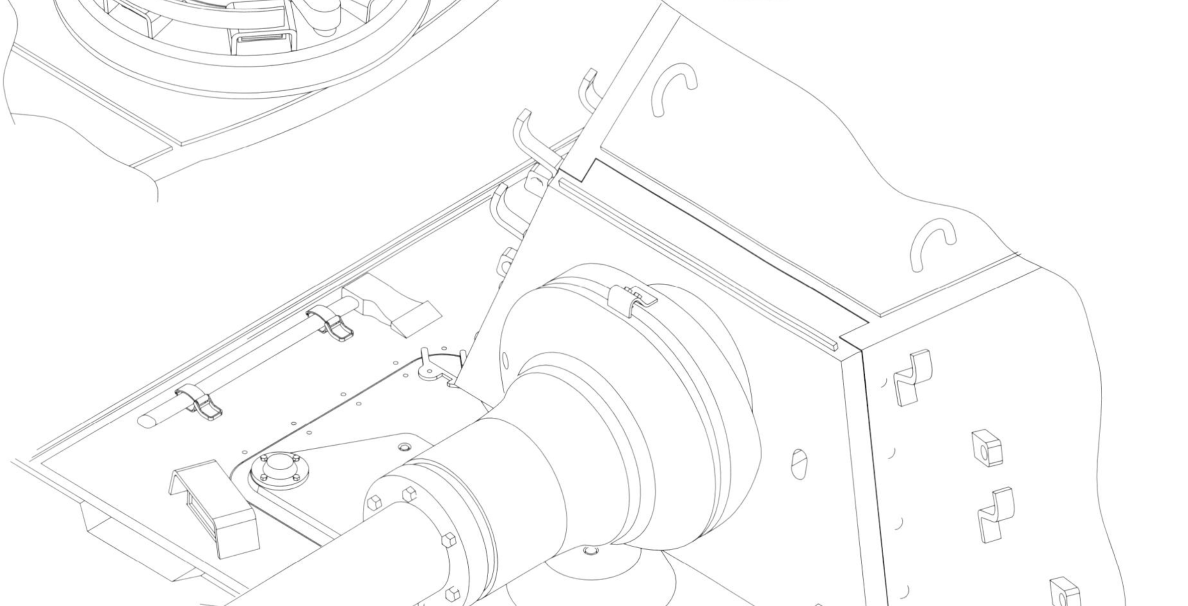

Henschel Turm details

Sheet 13

© Drawings by
Mariusz Suliga

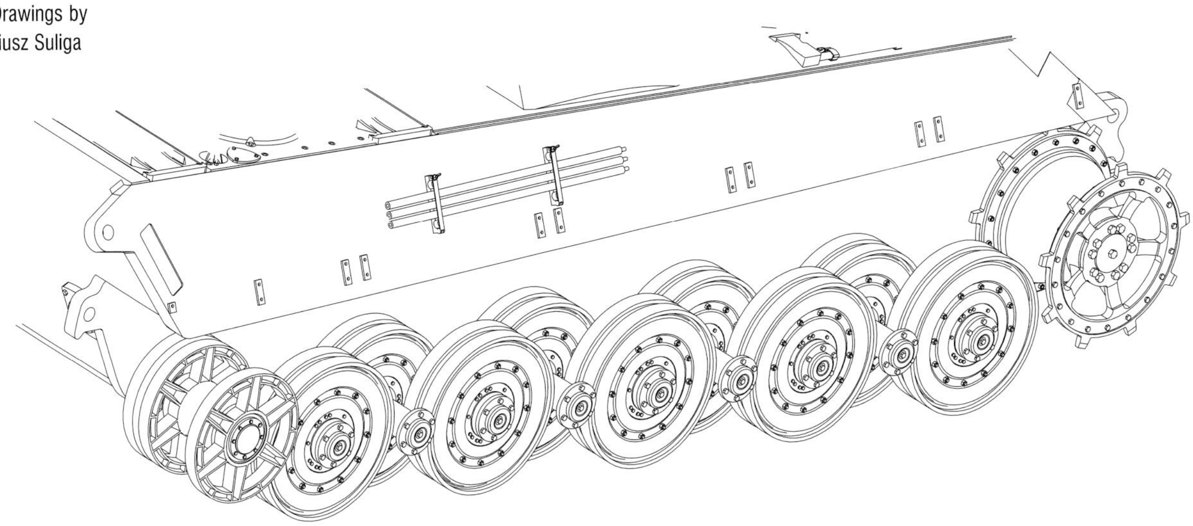

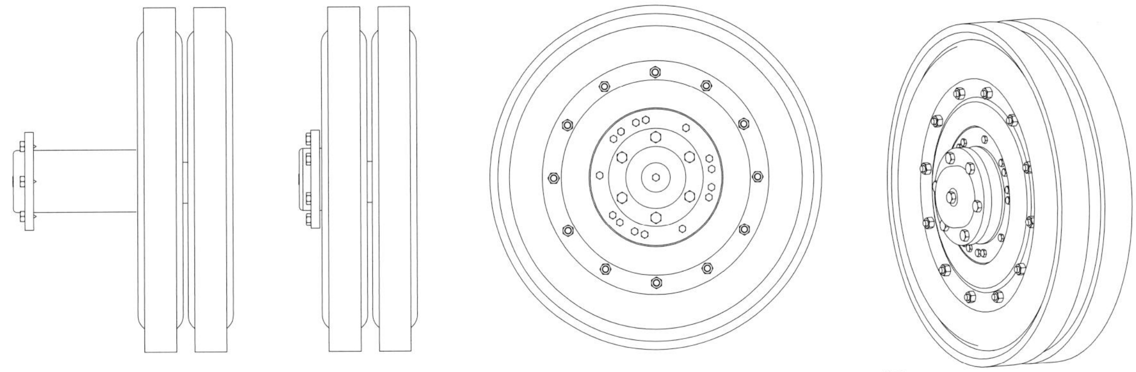

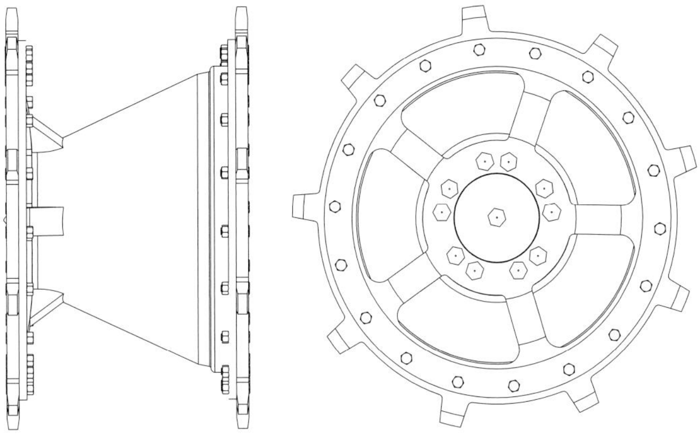

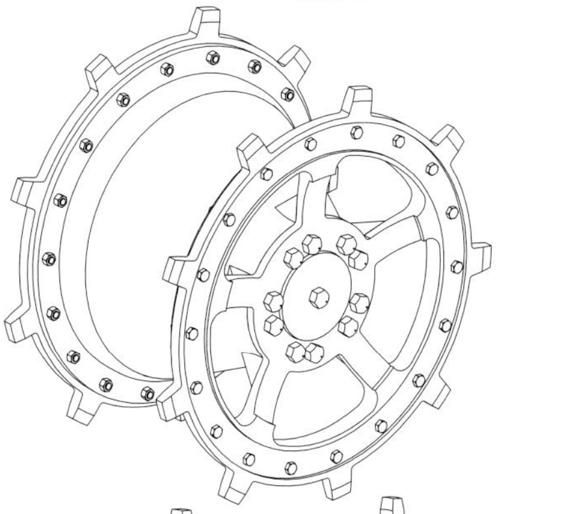

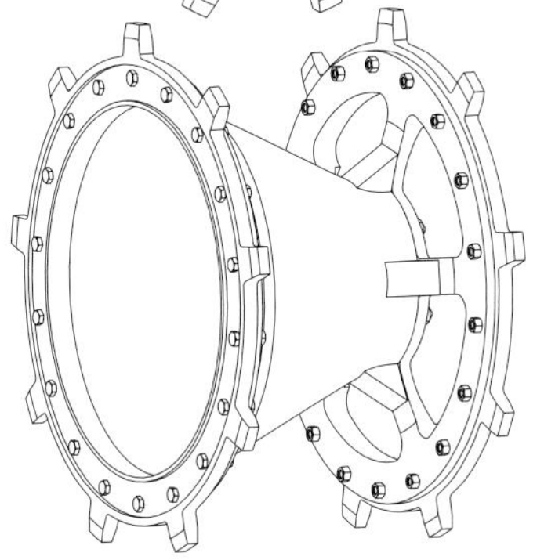

0   0.5   1m

1:17.5

Details of the chassis

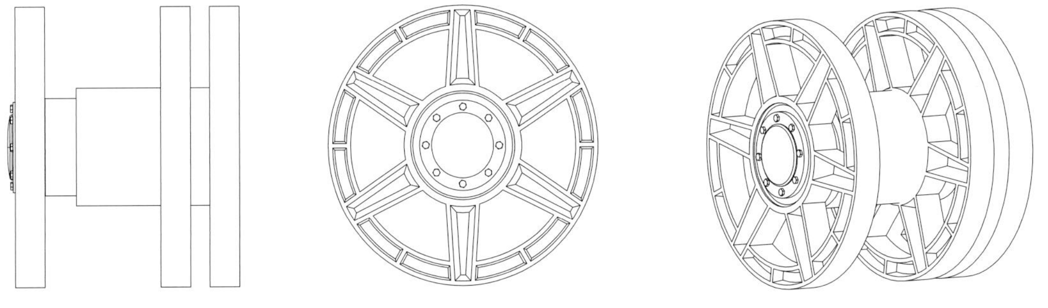

Sheet 14

© Drawings by
Mariusz Suliga

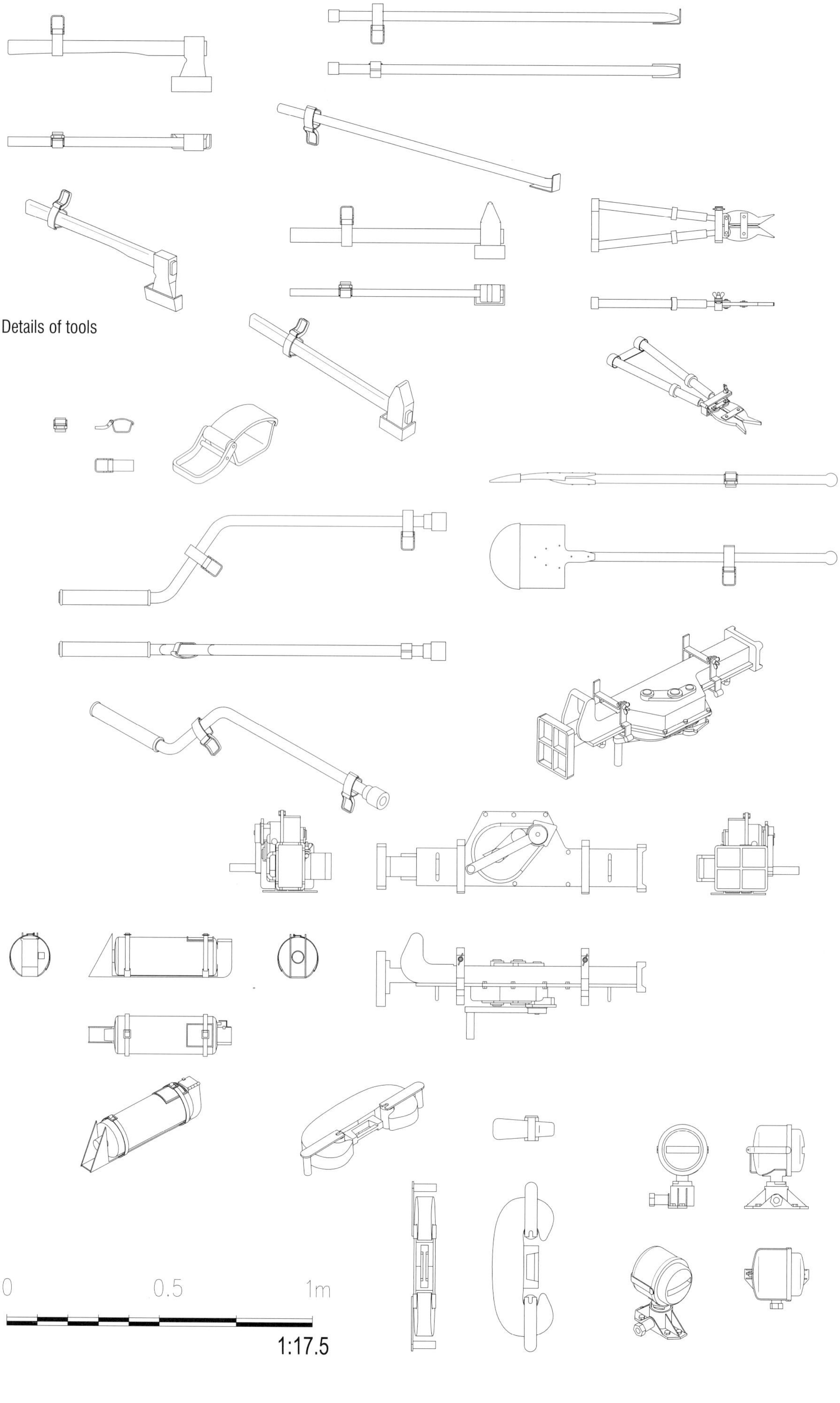

Details of tools

0   0.5   1m

1:17.5

Sheet 15

© Drawings by
Mariusz Suliga

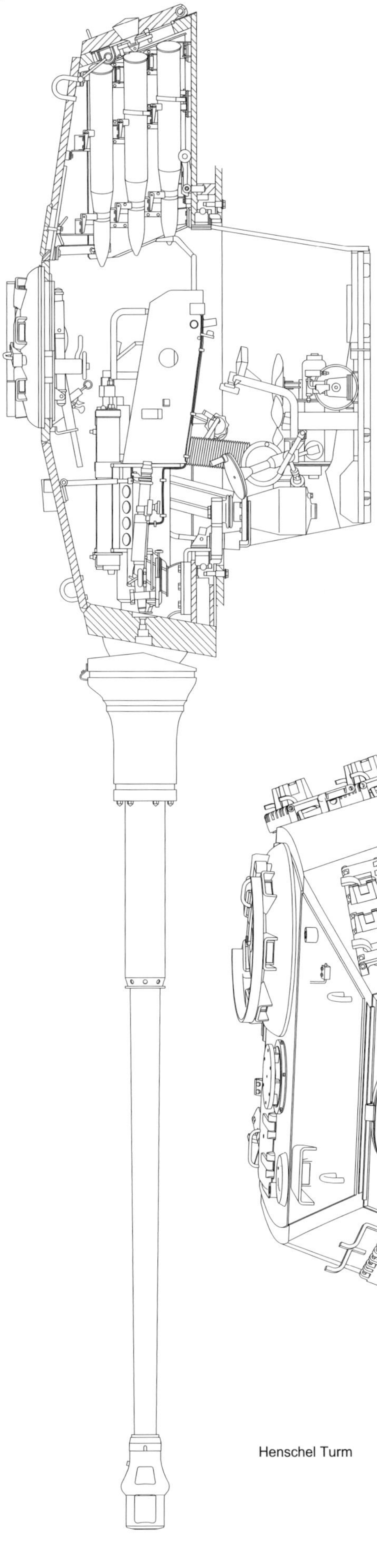

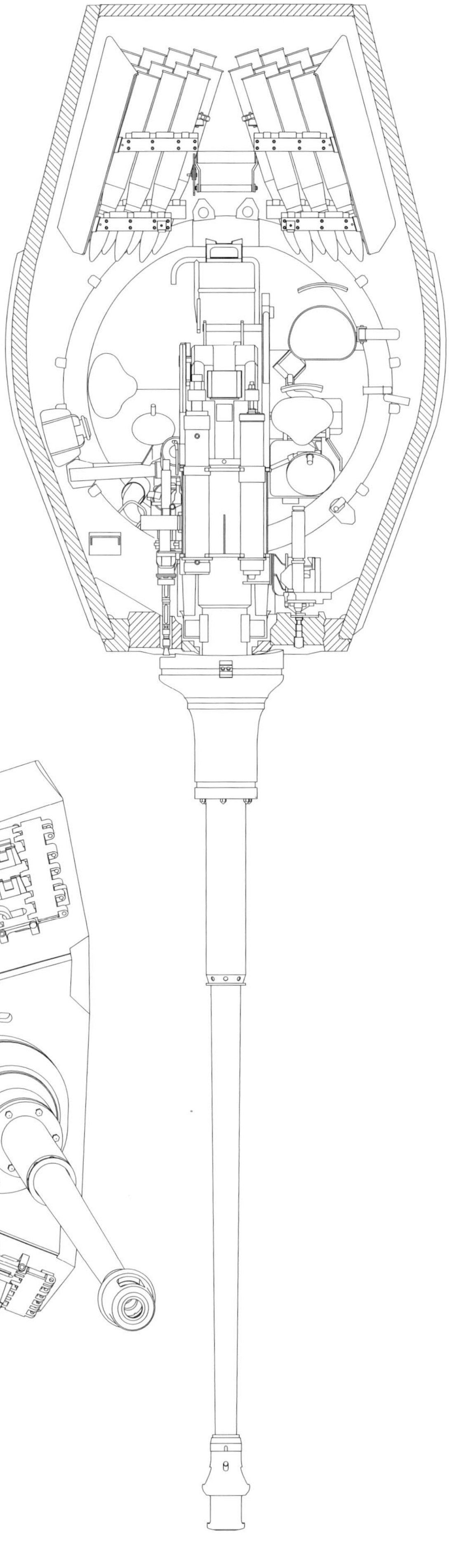

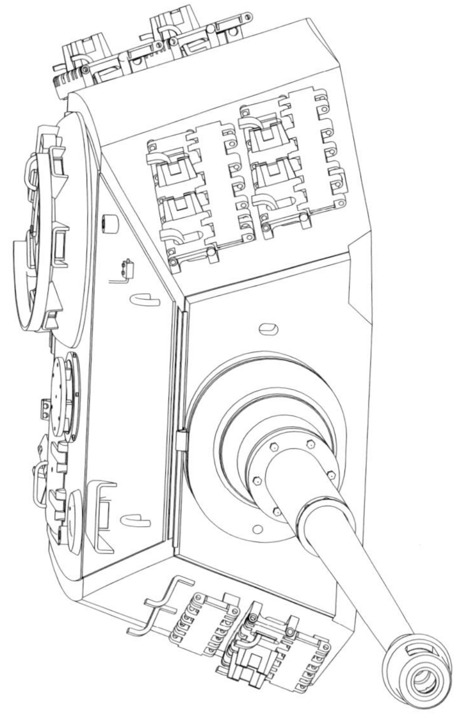

Henschel Turm

KAGERO

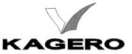

Sheet 16

© Drawings by
Mariusz Suliga

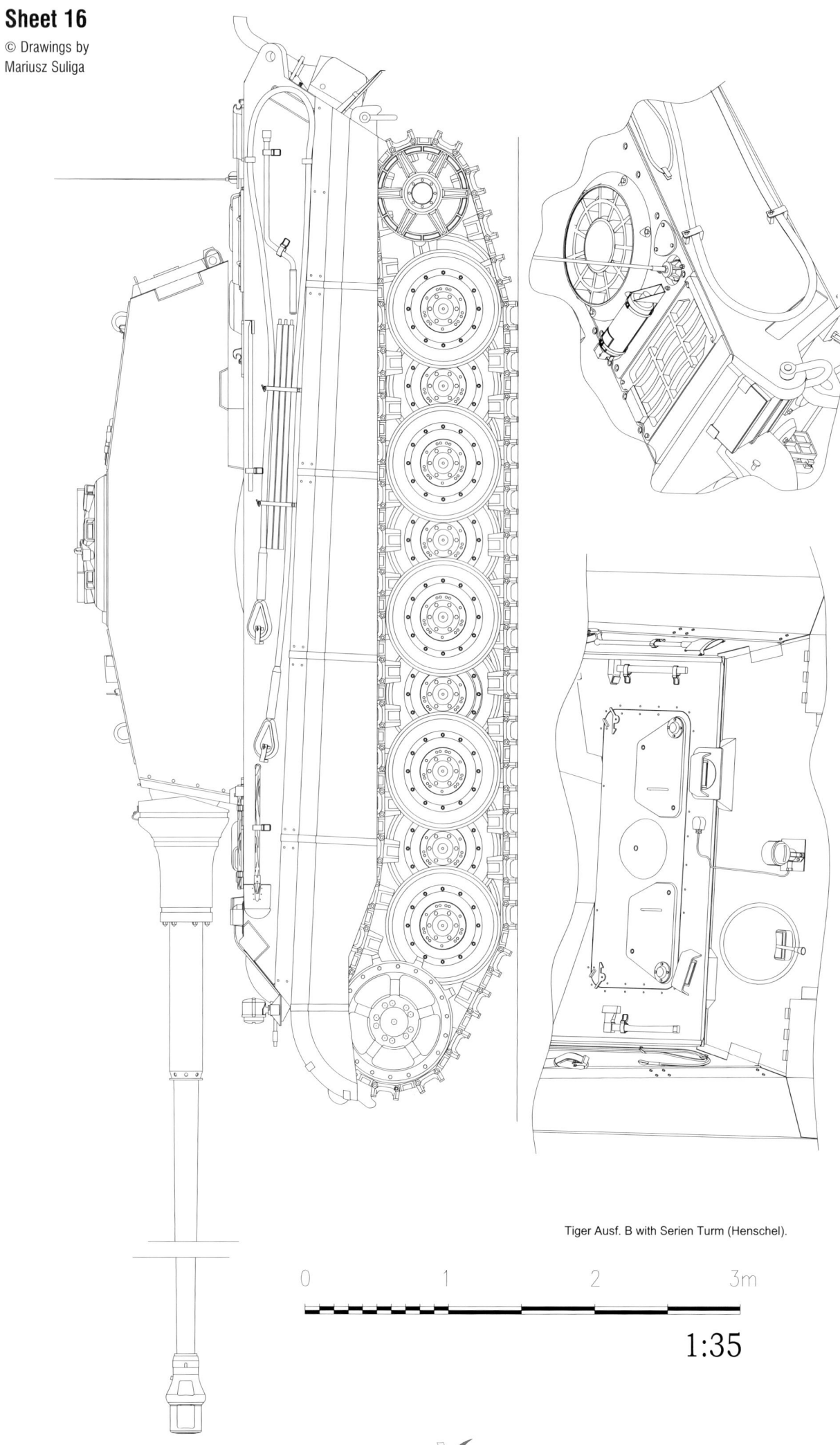

Tiger Ausf. B with Serien Turm (Henschel).

1:35

Sheet 17

© Drawings by
Mariusz Suliga

Tiger Ausf. B with Porsche turm completed in January 1944.

1:35

Sheet 18

© Drawings by
Mariusz Suliga

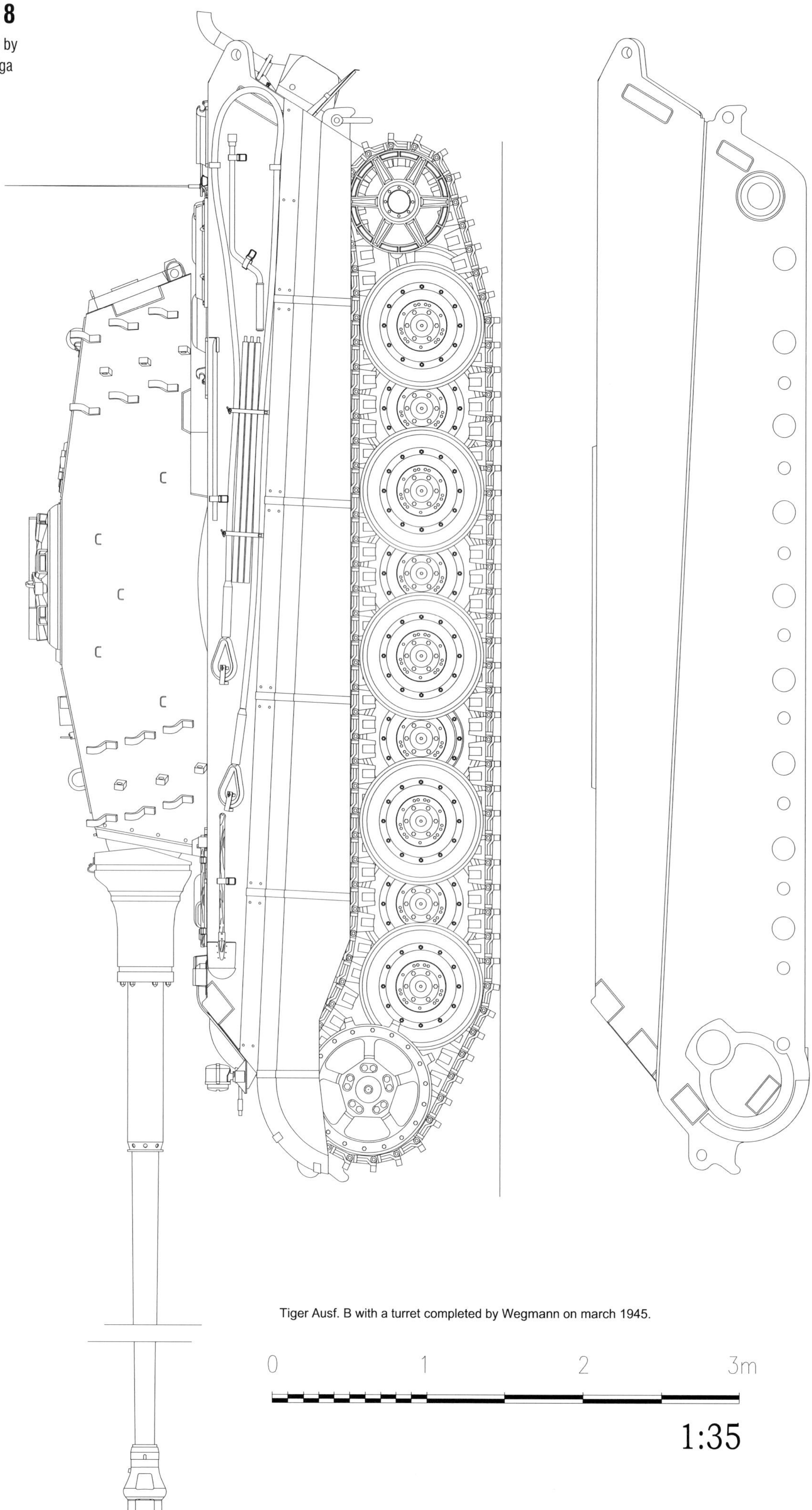

Tiger Ausf. B with a turret completed by Wegmann on march 1945.

0   1   2   3m

1:35

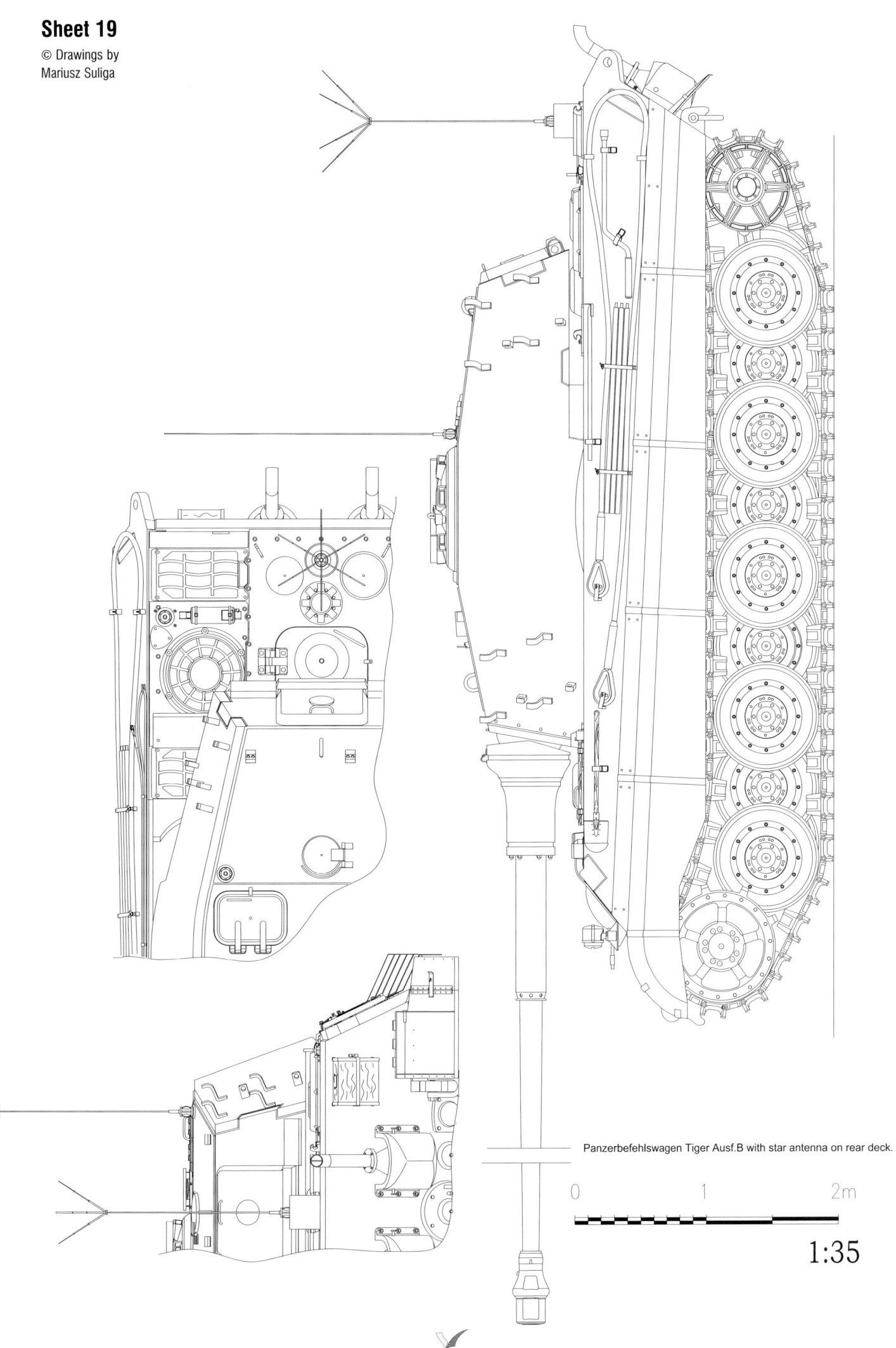
Panzerbefehlswagen Tiger Ausf.B with star antenna on rear deck.

Pz.Kpfw. VI Ausf. B with *Henschel Model* turret exhibited in *Munster Panzer Museum* (Germany). This vehicle with chassis number 280101 was originally put into service in *schwere SS Panzer Abteilung 501*. It was captured in the La Capelle area near French-Belgian border in September 1944. There were original tactical sings restored on the front armor plate. [Jacek Szafrański]

The *Kgs 24/800/300* combat tracks of *Königstiger* installed on the turret hangers which appeared not earlier than in July 1944. [Jacek Szafrański]

The *Pz.Kpfw. VI Ausf. B Kgs 24/800/300* combat track link. Note the 800-milimeters width of this element, which was the widest of mass-produced tracks dedicated to German tanks during World War Two. [Jacek Szafrański]

Pz.Kpfw. VI Ausf. B with *Henschel Model* turret exhibited in *Munster Panzer Museum* (Germany). This vehicle with chassis number 280101 was originally put into service in *schwere SS Panzer Abteilung 501*. It was captured in the La Capelle area near French-Belgian border in September 1944. There were original tactical sings restored on the front armor plate. [Jacek Szafrański]

The *Kgs 24/800/300* combat tracks of *Königstiger* installed on the turret hangers which appeared not earlier than in July 1944. [Jacek Szafrański]

The *Pz.Kpfw. VI Ausf. B Kgs 24/800/300* combat track link. Note the 800-milimeters width of this element, which was the widest of mass-produced tracks dedicated to German tanks during World War Two. [Jacek Szafrański]

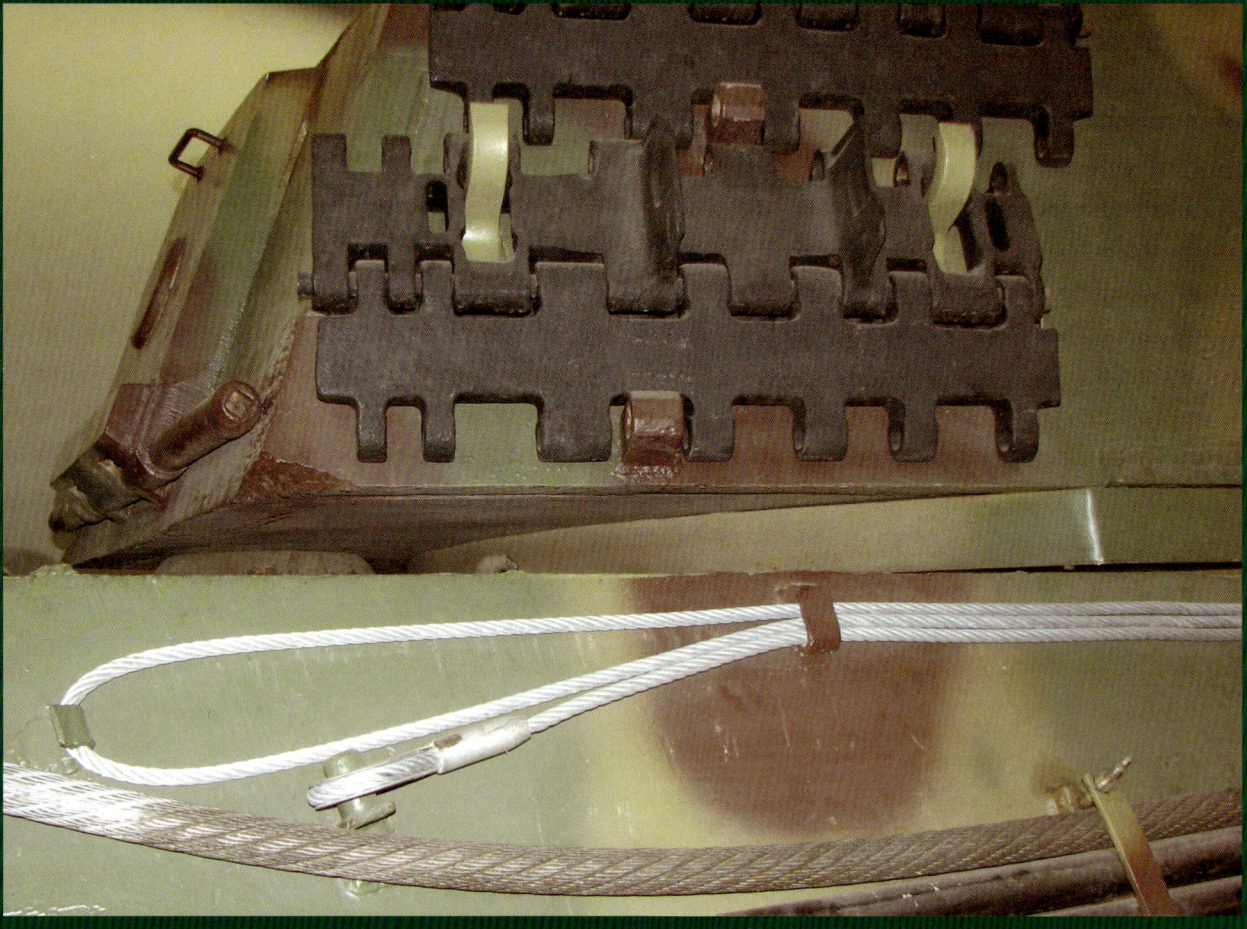

Panzer Museum Munster (Germany) *Königstiger* tracks and towing cable close up. [Jacek Szafrański]

Pz.Kpfw. VI Ausf. B exhibited in Munster tactical number. 321 indicates that the tank belonged to the 3rd Company of *schwere SS Panzer Abteilung 501*. [Jacek Szafrański]

Henschel Model Königstiger turret rear plate with the massive hatch. It was generally used for supplying the ammunition stowage. [Jacek Szafrański]

Front right corner of Munster *Pz.Kpfw. VI Ausf. B* chassis with fenders' mountings. [Jacek Szafrański]

Königstiger

Pz.Kpfw. VI Ausf. B Fahrgestell Nummer 280101 turret and chassis sides details. There is an external equipment including spade and towing cables installed on the armor clearly visible. [Jacek Szafrański]

Front left close up of Panzer Museum Munster *Königstiger* with spade and additional track links in the right place. Note the part of *schwere SS Panzer Abteilung 501* tactical sign painted in white. [Jacek Szafrański]

Pz.Kpfw. VI Ausf. B external *Kgs 24/800/300* track links hanging on the right sight of the *Henschel Model* turret. [Jacek Szafrański]

Close up of *Panzer Museum Munster Königstiger* engine compartment plate. [Jacek Szafrański]

Rear right view of *Pz.Kpfw. VI Ausf. B* exhibited in Munster, Germany. The cables and massive towing are visible. [Jacek Szafrański]

Another view of the rear right part of Munster Königstiger with exhaust pipes, C-shaped towing hooks and jack installed on the rear armor plate. [Jacek Szafrański]

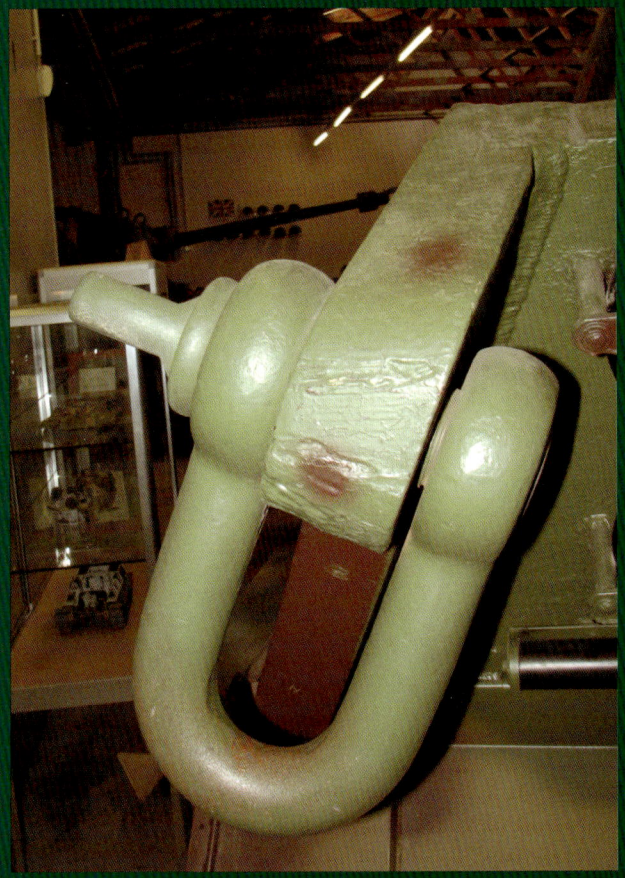

Rear towing of *Pz.Kpfw. VI Ausf. B* from *Panzer Museum Munster*. [Jacek Szafrański]

Right exhaust pipe of Munster *Königstiger*. This variant represents the serial-production one, slightly different than version installed in the *Pz.Kfpw. VI Ausf. B* prototypes. [Jacek Szafrański]

Königstiger   49

C-shaped hooks and massive towing of Munster *Pz.Kpfw. VI Ausf. B.* [Jacek Szafrański]

Panzer Museum Munster Königstiger left exhaust pipe. Note its massive base cover. [Jacek Szafrański]

Pz.Kpfw. VI Ausf. B – The Munster Panzer Museum

Lower part of Munster *Pz.Kpfw. VI Ausf. B* rear armor plate. This vehicle tracks represent the *Kgs 24/800/300* model. [Jacek Szafrański]

88 mm projectiles exhibited aside *Pz.Kpfw. VI Ausf. B* in Munester. There is a high-exhplosive *8.8 cm Srpenggranate 43* on the left and armor-piercing *8.8 cm Panzergranate 39/40* on the right. [Jacek Szafrański]

Warheads of Panzer Museum Munster *Königstiger*. The yellow one represents the high-explosive *8.8 cm Sprenggranate 43* with *A.Z. 23/28* base-detonating fuze, another one is *8.8. Panzergranate 39/40*. The latter armor-piercing destiny could be easily recognized by the white marking on the top. [Jacek Szafrański]

Pz.Kpfw. VI Ausf. B from Munster right drive sprocket. [Jacek Szafrański]

Rear part of the same tank suspension. The second external wheel is missing. [Jacek Szafrański]

Königstiger 53

Details of Munster *Königstiger* idler and road wheels. [Jacek Szafrański]

Pz.Kpfw. VI Ausf. B road whell having a diameter of 800 mm. [Jacek Szafrański]

Another view of *Panzer Museum Munster Pz.Kpfw. VI Ausf. B* right drive sprocket. [Jacek Szafrański]

Königstiger drive sprocket and road wheel close up. [Jacek Szafrański]

The 700 HP line V 12 *Maybach HL 230 P30* engine – the power plant of *Pz.Kpfw. VI Ausf B.* seen from different angles. The photos were made during its restoration process. [Mike Koenig]

Pz.Kpfw. VI Ausf. B – The Munster Panzer Museum

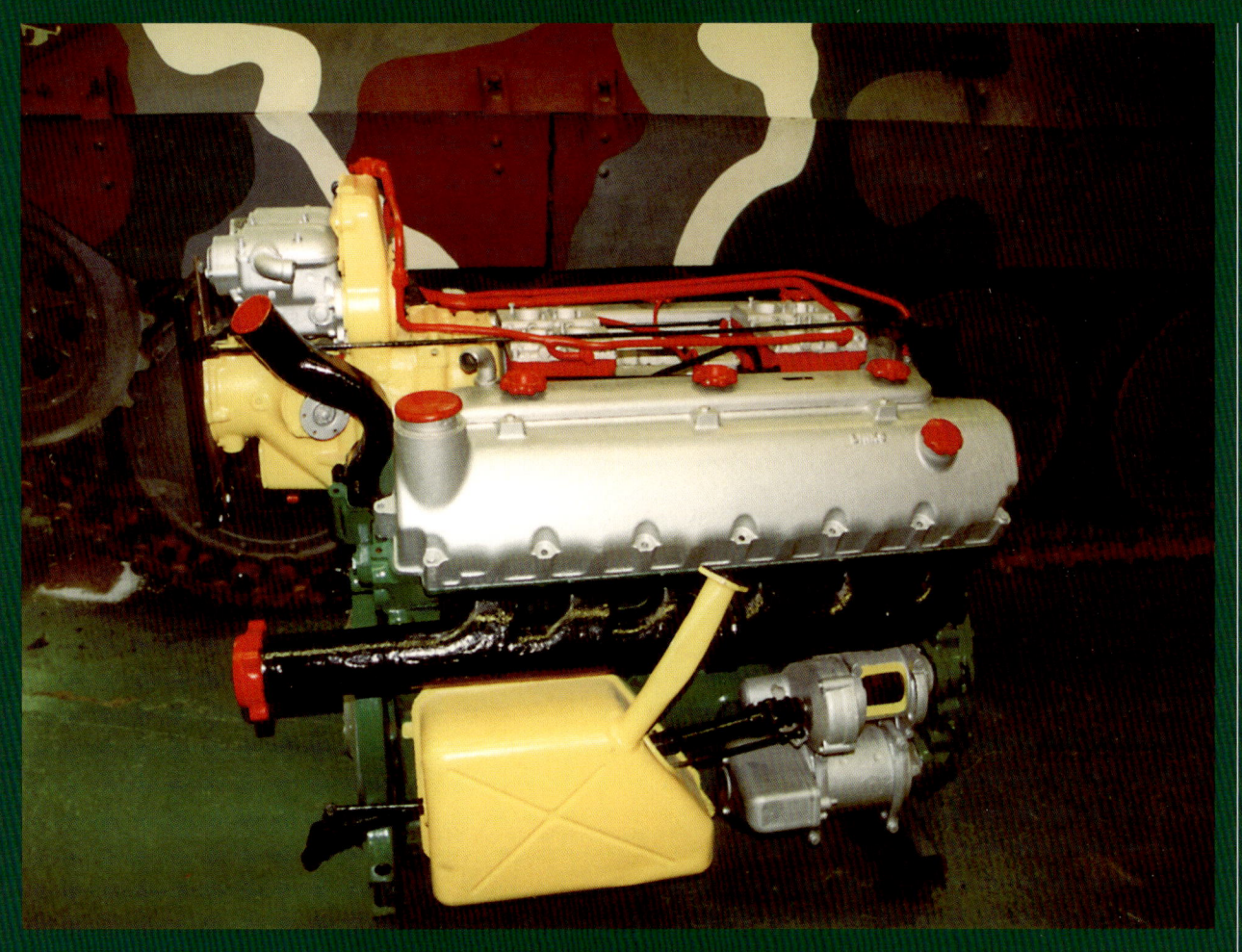

Königstiger 59

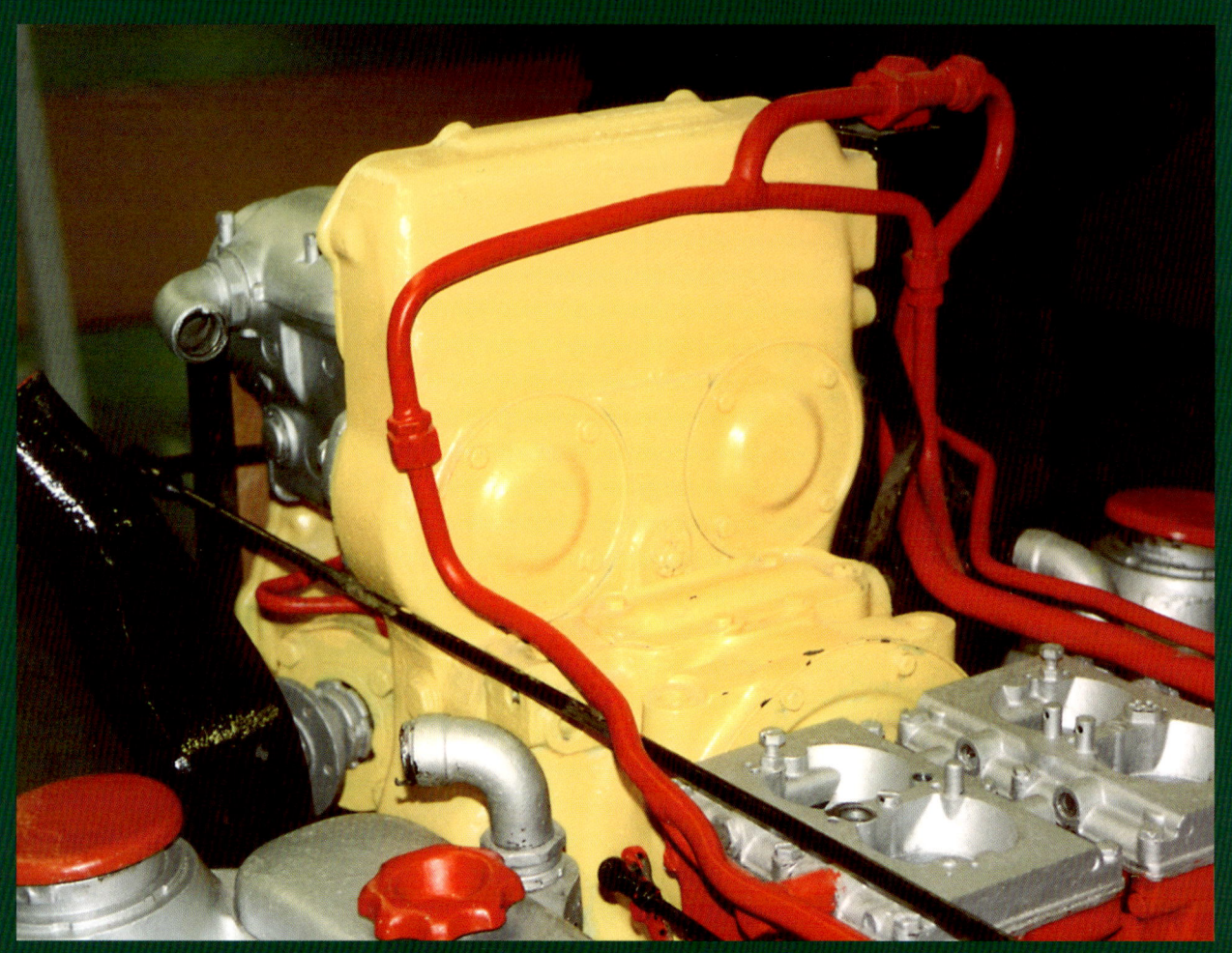

Pz.Kpfw. VI Ausf. B – The Tank Museum, Bovington

60 www.kagero.pl

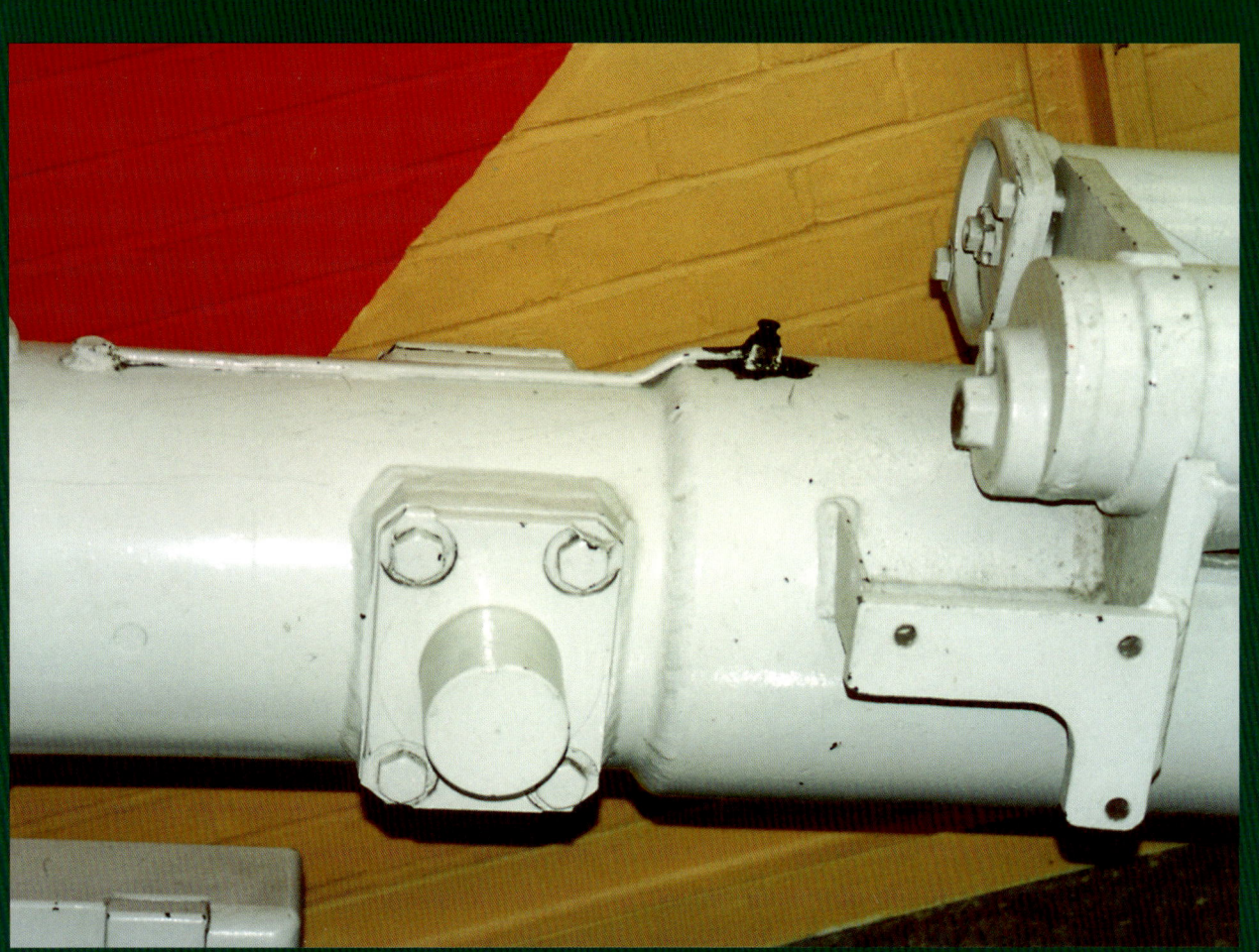

Königstiger main armament: *8.8 cm Kampfwagenkanone 43 L/71* barrel details with recoil system during restoration. This gun was one of the most effective used in combat during World War Two. [Mike Koenig]

Pz.Kpfw. VI Ausf. B – The Tank Museum, Bovington

Another view of *8.8 cm Kampfwagenkanone 43/71* recoil system. [Mike Koenig]

The massive two-chambered muzzle brake of *Pz.Kpfw. VI Ausf. B* main armament – *8.8 cm KwK 43 L/71* gun.

Pz.Kpfw. VI Ausf. B with *Porsche Model* turret exhibited in Royal Armored Corps Tank Museum Bovington (United Kingdom). This vehicle is the second *Königstiger* soft-steel prototype (*Versuchskonstruktion 2*) manufactured in Kassel, in December 1943. Its main armament is not original, it was installed during restoration process of the tank. [Mike Koenig]

Bovington *Königstiger Porsche Model* turret details. This version could be easily recognized by rounded front part, the commander cupola extending beyond the contour of the left side of the turret. [Mike Koenig]

Königstiger from Bovington front close up. The massive 100-milimeters thick gun mantlet is clearly visible. [Mike Koenig]

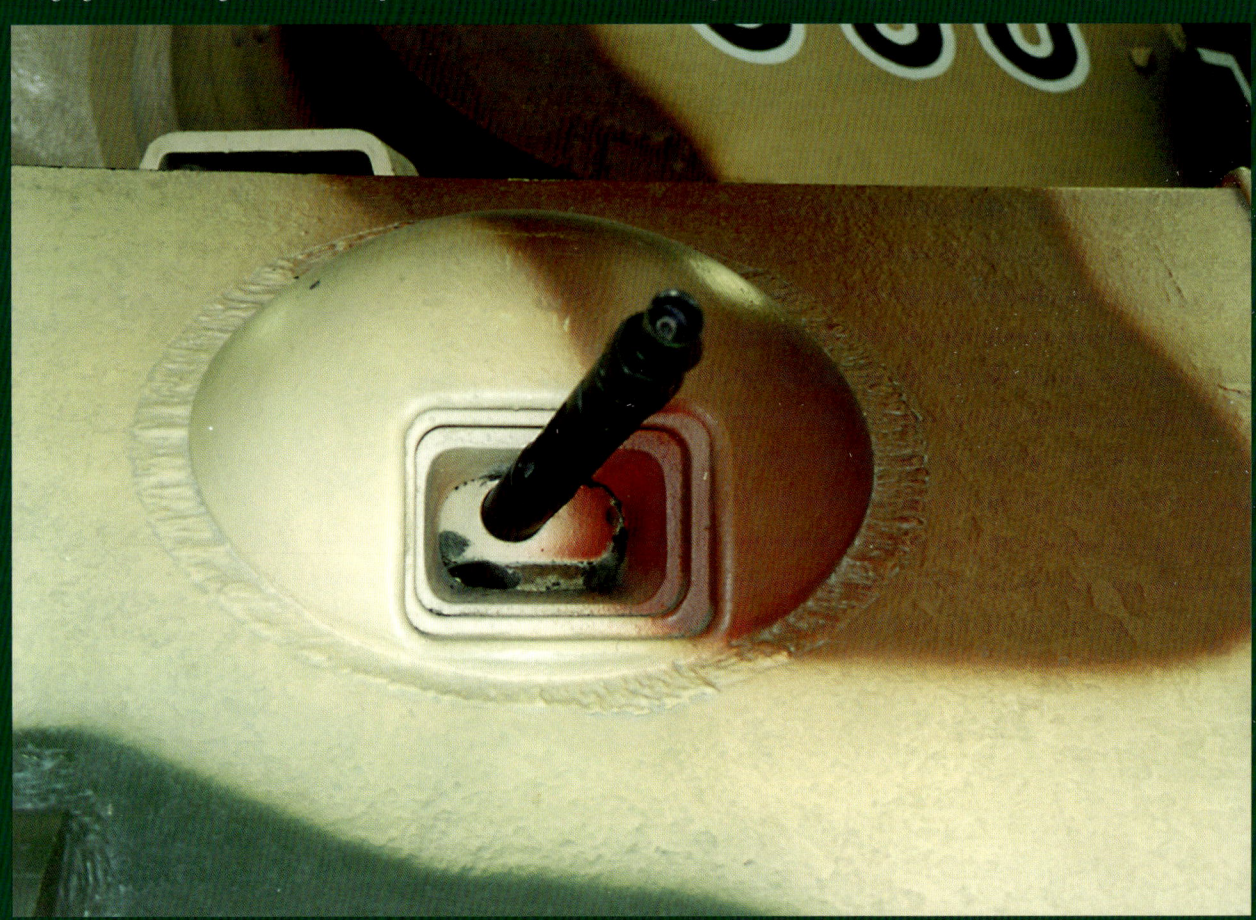

The machine gun spherical cupola installed in the front armor of every *Pz.Kpfw. VI Ausf. B*. It was identical to ones of *Pz.Kpfw. V Panther* medium tanks and armed with tank version of *7.92 mm Machinengewehr 34* as well. [Mike Koenig]

Details of Bovington *Königstiger* engine compartment right and top armor plate. [Mike Koenig]

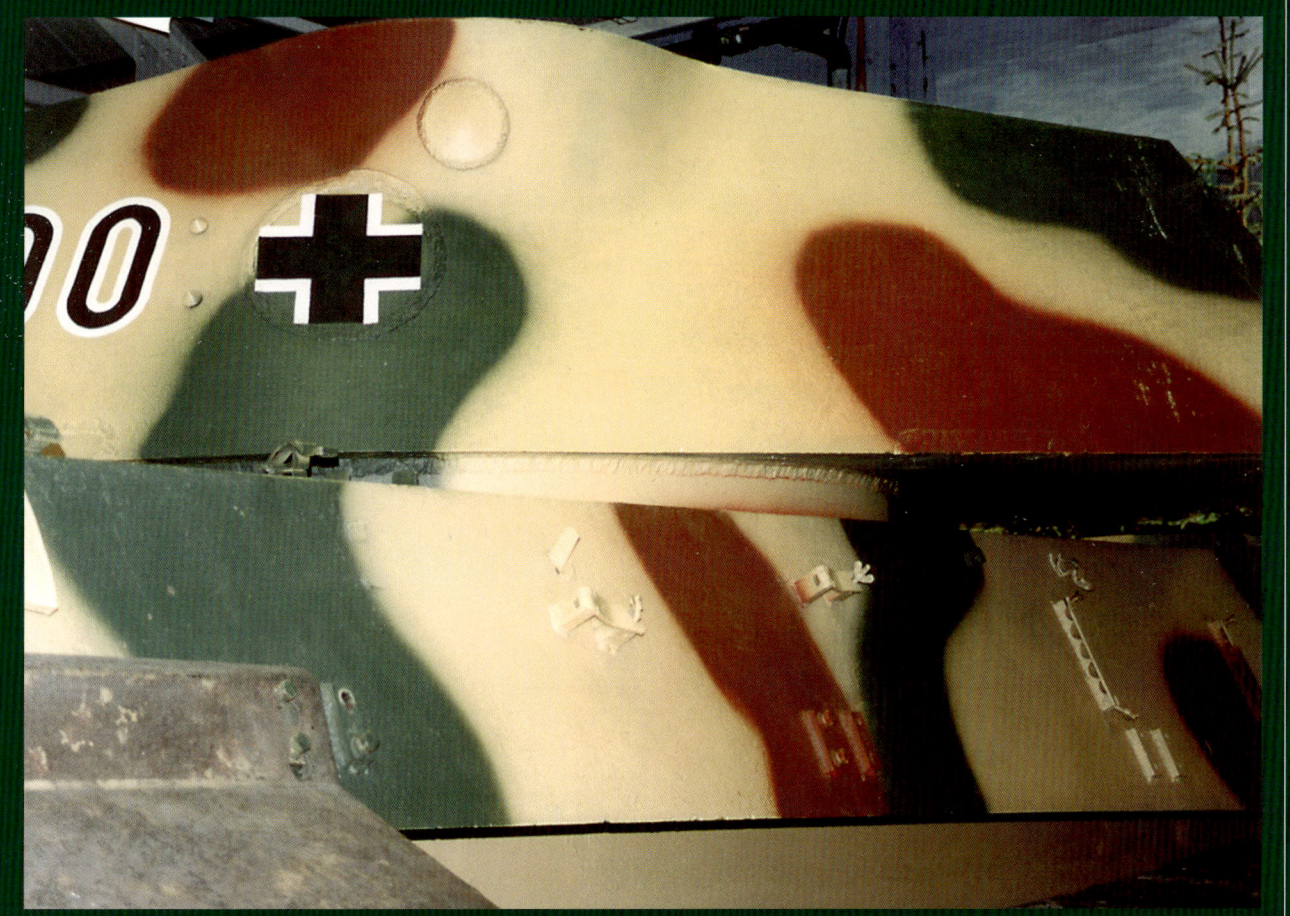

Left side of *Pz.Kpfw. VI Ausf. B* exhibited in the RAC Tank Museum turret and chassis. The vehicle external equipment is missing. There is a cover of the circular hole for throwing out the 88-milimeters shells visible above the black cross emblem. [Mike Koenig]

Rear part of Porsche Model turret of Bovington *Königstiger*. Note the massive plug in place of hatch installed in the serial-production tanks. [Mike Koenig]

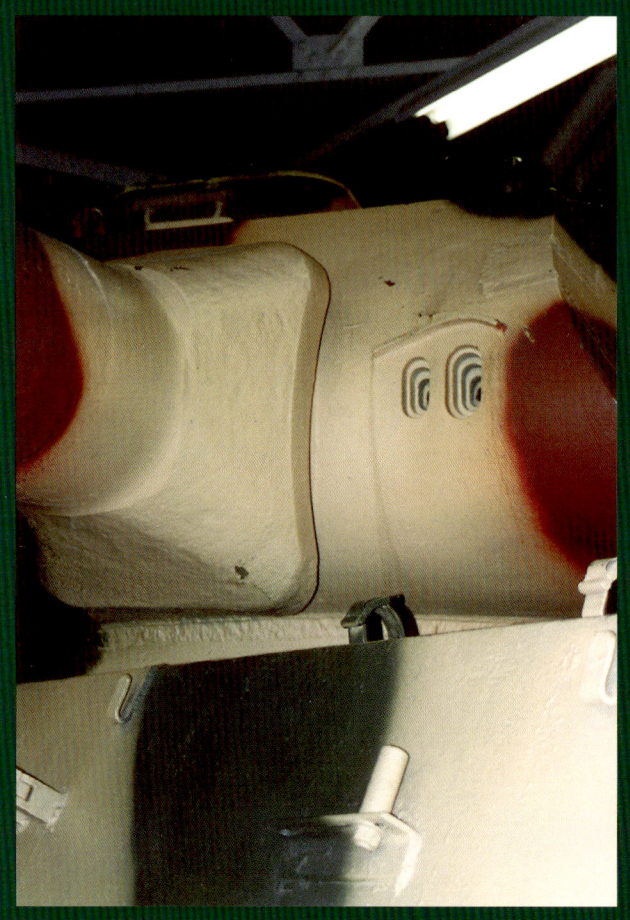

Left side of *Königstiger* from RAC Tank Museum with part of the fender preserved in its original condition. [Mike Koenig]

Bovington *Pz.Kpfw. VI Ausf. B* turret front armor close up with binocular *Turmzielfernrohr 9b/1* sighting telescope holes. [Mike Koenig]

Pz.Kpfw. VI Ausf. B with *Henschel Model* turret exhibited in front of the December 44 Museum in La Gleize (Belgium). This tank belonged to the 2nd Company of schwere SS Panzer Abteilung 501 which, as an element of Kampfgruppe Peiper, took part in the battle of the Bulge. This particular vechicle, bearing the tactical number of 213 was commanded by *SS-Sturmführer* Rudolf Dollinger and lost in the second half od December 1944 in the Wérimont Farm near La Gleize. There is a wrong color used in the tactical number filling. Instead of black it should be blue. Courtesy of members of SRH *Die Freiwilligen* and GRH *Panzer-Lehr* from Poland. [GRH *Panzer-Lehr*]

Rear armor plate of La Gleize *Königstiger*. [GRH *Panzer-Lehr*]

Another view of La Gleize *Königstiger*. The serial-production variant of exhaust pipes is clearly visible. [GRH *Panzer-Lehr*]

Königstiger

Pz.Kpfw. VI Ausf. B – The December 44 Museum, La Gleize

Rear right view of *Pz.Kpfw. VI Ausf. B* exhibited in La Gleize. The vehicle was restored but without any external equipment. [GRH *Panzer-Lehr*]

La Gleize *Königstiger* front armor close up with hit traces and *7.92 mm Maschinengewehr 34* cupola. [GRH *Panzer-Lehr*]

The hit trace of 75 mm anti-tank projectile in the middle weld of the front armor of La Gleize *Pz.Kpfw. VI Ausf. B*. [GRH *Panzer-Lehr*]

Front view of December 44 Museum *Pz.Kpfw. VI Ausf. B*. There are 800-milimeters wide *Kgs 24/800/300* combat track installed. Note the hit trace of the US Army 75 mm gun in the middle weld of the front plate. [GRH *Panzer-Lehr*]

Königstiger crewmen appearance

The *Panzerkampfwagen VI Ausf. B* crew's typical uniform was slightly as same as of dedicated to other *Panzerwaffe* armored vehicles. It usually consisted of introduced in the second half of thirties, black, woolen, fasten assimetrically, open-neck field jacket – *Feldjacke der Sonderbekleidung der Panzertruppen*, with a minor 1942 modifications connected with buttons and narrower collar. It was complemented with black woolen trousers, field or forage cap made of black cloth and black or brown laced shoes. There were also the herringbone twill summer variant of the German tanker uniform, almost identical to the cloth pattern excluding the capacious, so called *map* pockets on the jacket chest and one of the trousers legs. As far as the *Waffen-SS* units are concerned it was quite common to use the dot-pattern *Erbsentarnmuster* camouflage uniforms made of HBT material. Similar to them, the *Heer* officers sometimes wear the private-ordered uniforms in various shades of *Wehrmacht Splittertarnmuster*. There was also common to wear combat shorts and *Heereshemd* shirts especially during the warm months of summer 1944.

Field equipment of *Königstiger* crew members consisted only of the leather or, as it was quite common in the last months of World War Two, webbing main belt with 9 mm or 7.65 mm pistol holster. There were also not less than one *6x30 Dienstglas* or *10x50 Panzerglas* binoculars and *Modell 1935* map case in the heavy tank stowage dedicated to the tank commander. All of the crew members were also equipped with headphones and throat microphones.

Typical appearance of the *Heer* tank commander in 1944-1945 period. There are regular army armored weapon insignia – the *hussars skulls*, visible on the black, woolen field jacket and the soft officers cap with *Wehrmacht* insignia visible as well as leather officers belt with the open-type buckle. The soldier is equipped with another type of *10x50 Panzerglas* binoculars. [Bundesarchiv]

Waffen-SS tank crewman wearing herringbone twill, *Erbsentarnmuster 44* camouflage field jacket and trousers as well as black forage cap. This uniform variant was often used from 1944 especially in spring and summer months. The soldier's equimpment is reduced only to the leather main belt and pistol holster.

Painted by Arkadiusz Wróbel

SS-Unterscharführer of *schwere SS Panzer Abteilung 101*, Normandy, August 1944. His uniform consisted of black, woolen forage cap with *Waffen-SS* insignia, cloth field jacket, *Erbsentarnmuster 44* herringbone twill camouflage trousers and officers-type *Feldgrau* suede gloves. The soldier's equipment consists of the leather main belt with alloy buckle, *9 mm Pistole 08* holster, *10x50 Panzerglas* binoculars and headphones with a throat microphone set. There is also a map in celluloid cover visible. Reconstruction made by members of Stowarzyszenie Rekonstrukcji Historycznej *Die Freiwilligen* from Poland [Photo by Łukasz Dyczkowski Stowarzyszenie Niezależnych Fotoreporterów Tropiciel Historii].

SS-Sturmman of *schwere SS Panzer Abteilung 503*, Germany, April 1945. He is dressed in full tanker uniform made of woolen cloth and Modell 1944 black field cap with the late tape of *Waffen-SS BeVo* insignia. There is also a silk scarf visible on his neck, the common custom of World War Two German tankers. This *Königstiger* crew member equipment is reduced only to the leather main belt with steel buckle painted in silver, 7.95 Walther PPK holster and headphones with a throat microphone. Reconstruction made by members of Stowarzyszenie Rekonstrukcji Historycznej *Die Freiwilligen* from Poland [Photo by Łukasz Dyczkowski Stowarzyszenie Niezależnych Fotoreporterów Tropiciel Historii].

Camouflage and markings

During fifteen months of *Panzerkampfwagen VI Ausf. B* production, the tanks underwent several camouflage schemes modifications. According to archival photos, three *Königstiger* prototypes built in 1943, were painted only in dark yellow (*Wehrmacht Olive RAL 7028*) being sprayed over German military standard red oxide primer, in accordance with the directive applicable from February that year, changing the basic color of Third Reich military vehicles. Earlier, from the beginning of World War Two they were painted usually in dark grey (*Panzergrau RAL 7027*). Prepared in this way the *Royal Tigers* left the Kassel facility. Additional camouflage were painted by the crews after the transfer of tanks to their units.

By the summer of 1944, there were not any clear rules connected with the appearance of the camouflage schemes of *Pz.Kpfw. VI Ausf. B*. Usually, the vehicles were coated with wide patches in a combination of dark green (*Dunkelgrün RAL 6002*) and red brown (*Rotbrun RAL 8017*), or only one of these colors. Finally, there was a directive issued on August 19 under which the prior to being shipped from factory all vehicles needed to have new *Hiterhalt-Tarnung* (*Ambush* type) camouflage scheme applied. It consisted of patches of olive green (*Olivgrün RAL 6003*) and red brown (*Rotbrun RAL 8017*) sprayed over dark yellow (*Wehrmacht Olive RAL 7028*) background. The darker shades were complemented by small, dark yellow and green dots. It is worth to mention, that from September 1944 dark brown patches had been increasingly replaced by leaving the red oxide primer. The mono-tone *Wehrmacht Olive* factory-applied variant were restored in October. That time, in case of lack of dark yellow paint, there were the dark green shades approved as a vehicle painting base.

Another modification was introduced in December 1944, when the base color become dark green. During the winter campaigns, many vehicles in whole or in part were painted white, washable paint or lime. The first camouflage variant was adopted, among others, in fighting in Poland *schwere Heeres Panzer Abteilung 501*, or, deployed at the time in Hungary, *schwere Heeres Panzer Abteilung 503*. The second variant was represented by also operating by the Balaton Lake, *schwere Heeres Panzer Abteilung 509*.

There were some uniusal, very original *Königstiger* camouflage schemes appeared on the front line in the final stage of Adolf Hitler's state. An example of this was at least one tank belonging to *schwere Heeres Panzer Abteilung 511* (re-designated in January 1945, *schwere Heeres Panzer Abteilung 502*), fighting against the Red Army in East Germany, spring 1945. It was coated with so called octopus painting, consisted of a large, dark yellow spots on dark green background, which was enriched with dark green circles. It cannot be excluded that in the final period of the *King Tiger* production, tanks with a mono-tone red oxide primer paint could have been sent to the frontline as well.

At the same time the external paint colors were modified, there was a change in the interior scheme of *Pz.Kpfw. VI Ausf. B*. In August 1944, the ivory paint (*Elfenbien*) dedicated to all *Panzerwaffe* combat vehicles was replaced by red oxide primer.

A notable issue is the analysis of markings catalogue which appeared on *Pz.Kpfw. VI Ausf. B* tanks sent to the combat units. The basic symbol painted usually on the turret side was was a black cross with white outline (*Balkenkreuz*) – the mark of German or specifically: Third Reich nationality. Besides, according to the system generally adopted in *Panzerwaffe*, *King Tigers* usually bear the three-digit tactical numbers, located on the side of the turret too. The first cipher referred to a company number, the second – the platoon number, while the third – the vehicle itself. Most often they were painted using templates after transferring the tank to a combat unit. Earlier, as suggested by archival photographs, during proving ground tests, there were a handwritten test numbers, usually black and inscribed in the oval, painted on the front armor plate.

The colors of tactical numbers varied. They met both the typical red or black numbers with a typical white outline, and its lack or, as in the case of fighting in August, in northern France, *schwere SS Panzer Abteilung 101*, yellow or as in some tanks send to the Balaton front in 1945, only blue. An interesting and rare method was adopted in case of *Waffen-SS Royal Tigers* during the battle of the Bulge. In that case, colors of tactical numbers color symbolized the company affiliation: black assigned to the 1st Company, red – 2nd Company, and blue – 3rd Company and staff section of *schwere SS Panzer Abteilung 501*. In the last subunit there were three *Königstiger*, bearing the tactical numbers: 007, 008 and 009 outlined either in white or light shade of yellow.

There were also vehicles representing unusual combinations of ciphers sent to the front line. *Pz.Kpfw. VI Ausf. B* tanks assigned in the early summer 1944 to *Funklenk Panzer Kompanie 316* presented white, hand-painted double-digit numbers of almost the entire tower height, in two cases, beginning with the digit 0: 02 and 03. Other interesting numerical marking was met in the ranks of *schwere Heeres Panzer Abteilung 505*, in 1945 deployed

Table 4. *Pz.Kpfw. VI Ausf. B* heavy tank camouflage schemes modifications

January	1944	Introducing the mono-tone dark yellow factory-applied background.
August	1944	Introducing the Ambush factory-applied camouflage. Replacing the ivory interior paint with red oxide primer one.
September	1944	Replacing the red brown patches with red oxide primer ones.
October	1944	Restoring the mono-tone dark yellow factory-applied background
December	1944	Substituting the mono-tone dark yellow factory-applied background by the dark green one.

to East Prussia. They were painted in two blocks on the side of the barrel. In case of vehicles belonged to *schwere Heeres Panzer Abteilung 506*, the numbers were separated by *Balkenkreuz*. The 505th independent heavy tank battalion was also distinguished by the big unit emblem, painted on the side of the turret. It was called *Ritter* and represented a charging knight.

As far as method for determining the tactical association of the Royal Tigers is concerned, the campaign symbols are also worth to be mentioned. One of them are connected with the *Unternehmen Herbstnebel* – the German counter offensive in Ardennes and particularly, the *Waffen-SS Königstiger* in December 1944. According to Steven Zaloga and the archival materials invoked, there were *Rollbahn D* inscription applied on the front armor of some of *Kampfgruppe Peiper* heavy tanks. This marking was connected with the unit's combat route. An additional role of crews of these *Pz.Kpfw. VI Ausf. B*s would have been to help in the traffic-control tasks. The 501st SS heavy tank battalion adopted also the custom of painting the unit emblem above one of the front fenders. It was a white shield with crossed keys, located above a pair of oak leaves.

Acknowledgments

Kagero Publishing would like to thank Mr Jacek Szafrański, through whom posting of Panzer Museum Munster and RAC

Panzerkampfwafen VI Ausf. B tanks of schwere Heeres Panzer Abteilung 501 being repaired on the Vistula Front. August 1944. [Kagero Archive]

One of the last production series (March 1945) *Pz.Kpfw. VI Ausf. B* of *schwere Heeres Panzer Abteilung 511* photographed in the Holzhausen Area, 1945. [Kagero Archive]

Table 5. Pz.Kpfw. VI Ausf. B aces.

		Unit	Confirmed victories
1.	Kurt Knispel	s.Heeres.Pz.Abt 503	168
2.	Paul Egger	s.SS.Pz.Abt 102 (502)	113
3.	Heinz Rondorf	s.Heeres.Pz.Abt 503	106
4.	Heinz Gärtner	s.Heeres.Pz.Abt 503	103
5.	Karl Körner	s.SS.Pz.Abt 103 (503)	102
6.	Möbius Rolf	s.SS.Pz.Abt 101 (501)	101
7.	Will Fey	s.SS.Pz.Abt 102 (502)	88
8.	Karl Bromann	s.SS.Pz.Abt 103 (503)	66
9.	Richard Freiherr von Rosen	s.Heeres.Pz.Abt 503	25
10.	Franz Staudegger	s.SS.Pz.Abt. 101 (501)	22

Tank Museum Bovington *Pz.Kpfw. VI Ausf. B* tanks photos was possible. Separate thanks we would like to send to Mr Krzysztof Hartung from Stowarzyszenie Rekonstrukcji Historycznej *Die Freiwilligen* (Poland) for lending the La Gleize *Königstiger* photo set as well to all members of this organization, whose *Panzerwaffe* soldiers silhouettes are part of this book. We would like to thank also Mr Łukasz Dyczkowski from Stowarzyszenie Niezależnych Fotoreporterów Tropiciel Historii (Poland), the author of reenacting photos of *Panzerwaffe* soldiers issued here.

Selected bibliography

Archer L., *Panzerwrecks. German Armor 1944-1945*, Issue 10, New York 2009.
Bishop C., *German Panzers in World War II*, Stroud 2008.
Chamberlain P., *Encyclopedia of German Tanks od World War Two*, London 1999.
Green M., *Tiger tanks at war*, St. Paul 2008.
Hormann J., *Uniforms of the Panzer Troops 1917 – to the Present*, West Chester 1989
Jentz T., *Germany's Tiger Tanks: Tiger I & II: Combat Tactics*, Atglen 2007.
Jentz T., *Kingtiger Heavy Tank 1942-1945*, London 1994.
Jentz T., *Panzertruppen. The Complete Guide to the Creation & Combat Employment of Germany's Tank Force 1943-1945*, Atglen 1996.
Krawczyk W., *Army Panzer Uniforms in Colour Photographs*, Moscow.
Pallud J-P., *Ardennes 1944: Peiper and Skorzeny*, London 1988.
Steinhardt F., Rubbel A., *The Combat History of schwere Panzer Abteilung 503. In Action in the East and West with Tiger I and II*, Winnipeg 2000.
Schneider W., *Tiger im Kampf Band 3. Die Einsätze in Normandie*, Berlin 2005.
Schneider W., *Tigers in Combat*, vol. I and vol. II, Mechanicsburg 2004-2005.
Spielberger W., *Die Panzer-Kampfwagen Tiger und seine Abarten*, Stuttgart 1998.
Williamson G., *Panzer Crewman 1939-1945*, Oxford 2002.
Zaloga S., *The Battle of the Bulge*, Hong Kong 2001.

Pz.Kpfw. VI Ausf. B belonged probably to the 1st Company of schwere *SS Panzer Abteilung 101* destroyed in France, summer 1944. [Kagero Archive]

Painted by Arkadiusz Wróbel

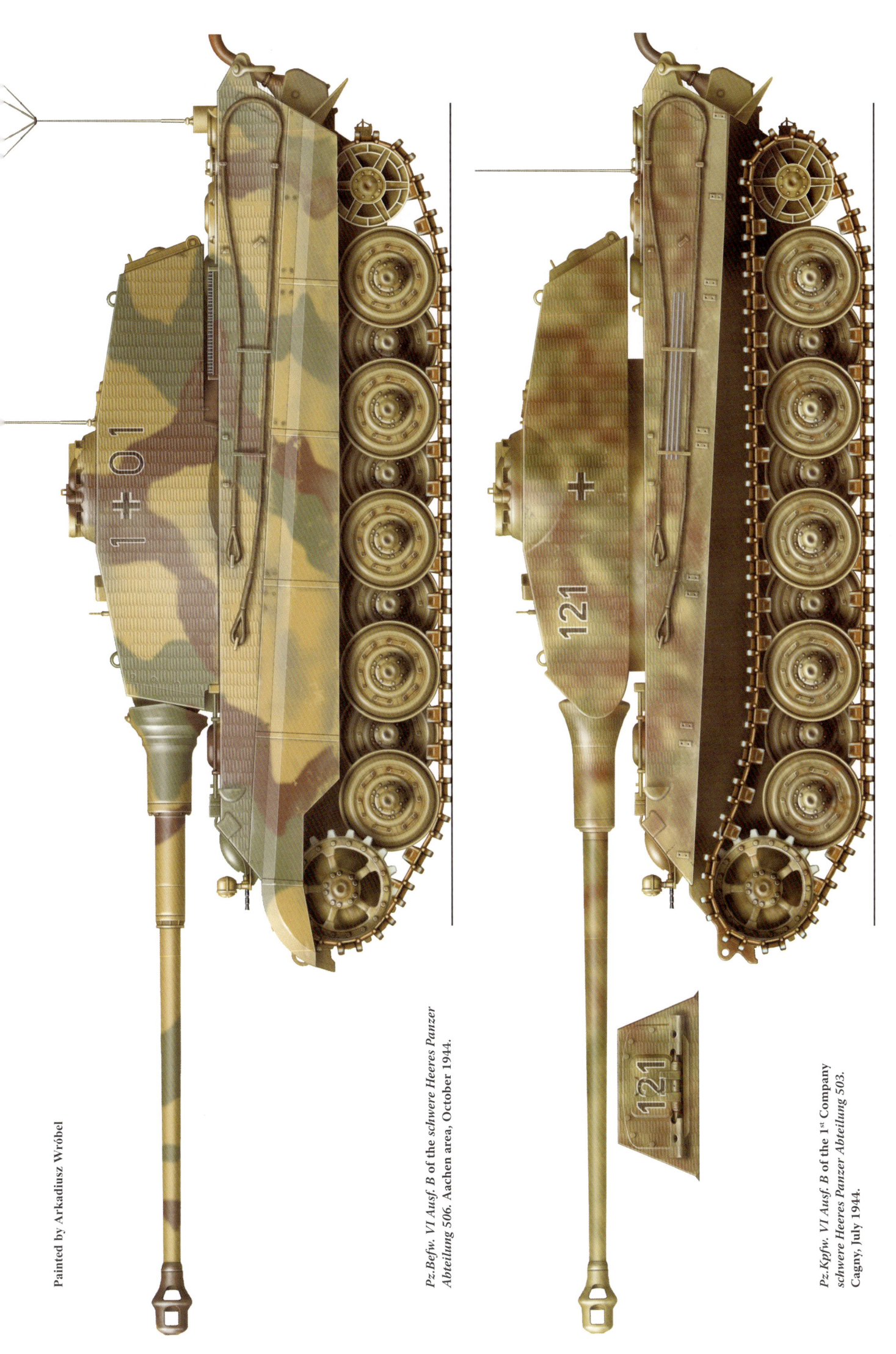

Pz.Befw. VI Ausf. B of the schwere Heeres Panzer Abteilung 506. Aachen area, October 1944.

Pz.Kpfw. VI Ausf. B of the 1st Company schwere Heeres Panzer Abteilung 503. Cagny, July 1944.

Painted by Arkadiusz Wróbel

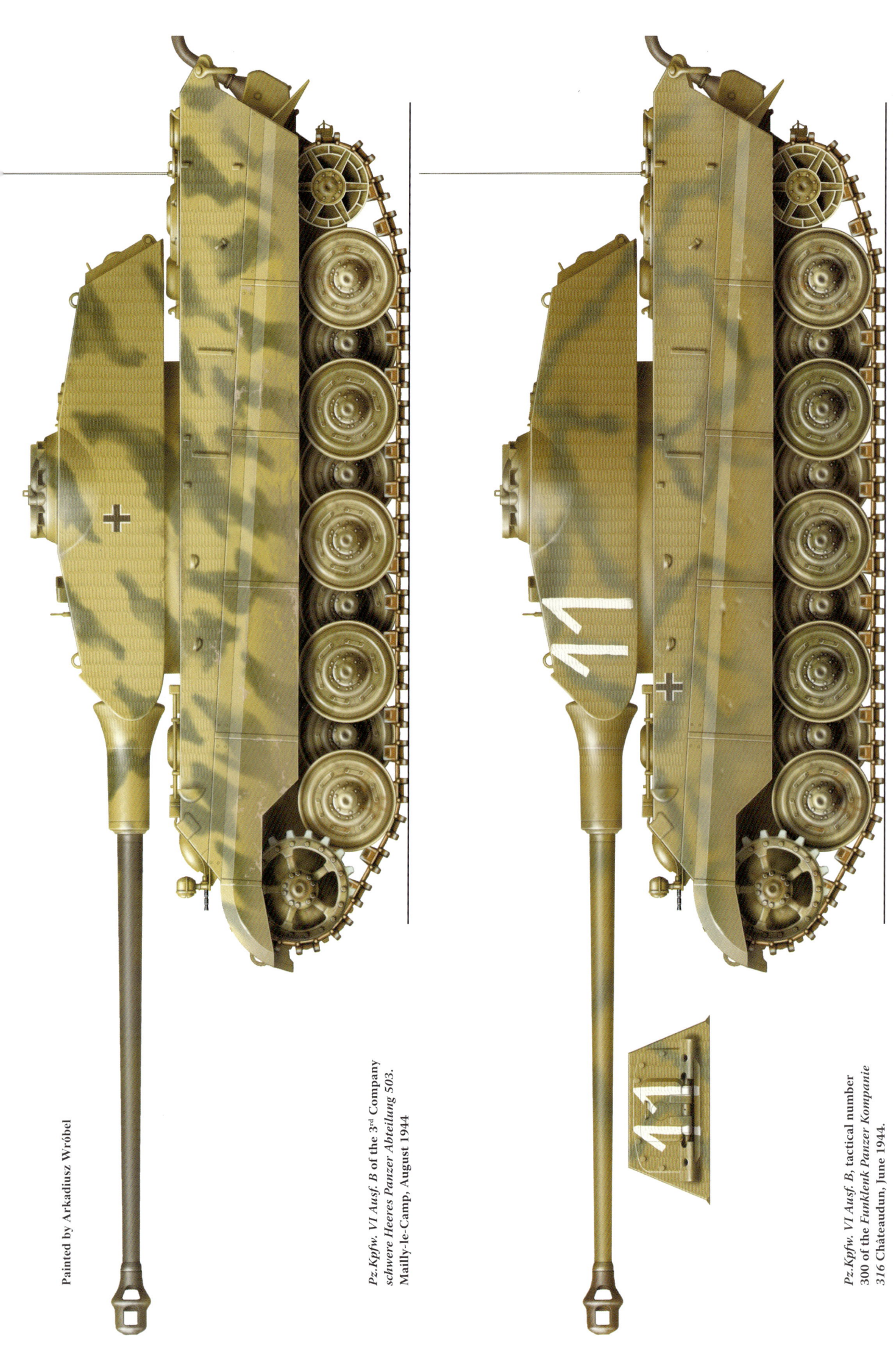

Pz.Kpfw. VI Ausf. B of the 3rd Company schwere Heeres Panzer Abteilung 503. Mailly-le-Camp, August 1944

Pz.Kpfw. VI Ausf. B, tactical number 300 of the *Funklenk Panzer Kompanie* 316 Châteaudun, June 1944.

Painted by Arkadiusz Wróbel

Pz.Kpfw. VI Ausf. B, probably of the Staff Company schwere Heeres Panzer Abteilung 503. Sennelager, September 1944.

Pz.Kpfw. VI Ausf. B, tactical number 313 of the 3rd Company schwere Heeres Panzer Abteilung 501. Sandomierz bridgehead, August 1944.

Painted by Arkadiusz Wróbel

Pz.Kpfw. VI Ausf. B, tactical number 300 of the 3rd Company schwere Heeres Panzer Abteilung 503 commander. Mailly-le-Camp, August 1944.

Pz.Kpfw. VI Ausf. B, tactical number 101 of schwere SS Panzer Abteilung 503. Berlin, April/May 1945.

Painted by Arkadiusz Wróbel

Pz.Kpfw. VI Ausf. B, tactical number 133 of the 1st Company of schwere SS Panzer Abteilung 101. France, September 1944.

Pz.Befw. VI Ausf. B, tactical number I of schwere Heeres Panzer Abteilung Feldherrnhalle. Czech Republic, May 1945.

Painted by Arkadiusz Wróbel

Pz.Kpfw. VI Ausf. B, tactical number 213 of the 2nd Company of *schwere Heeres Panzer Abteilung 509*. Hungary, winter 1944/1945.

Pz.Befw. VI Ausf. B, tactical number 502 of *schwere Heeres Panzer Abteilung 501*. Poland, summer 1944.

Painted by Arkadiusz Wróbel

Pz.Kpfw. VI Ausf. B, tactical number 122 of the 1st Company of *schwere Heeres Panzer Abteilung Feldherrnhalle*. Hungary, spring 1945.

Pz.Kpfw. VI Ausf. B, tactical number 331 of the 3rd Company of *schwere SS Panzer Abteilung 501* commander, Rolf von Westernhagen. Hungary, spring 1945.

KAGERO.EU

Free magazines in download section
Kagero's Publication 2014 Catalogue

READ FOR FREE
on KAGERO's Area

LIST OF PUBLICATION SERIES

TopColors

- Messerschmitt Bf 109G Over Germany
- Fighters over Japan
- Eastern Front
- Supermarine Spitfire Mk VIII
- Messerschmitt Bf 109 F

miniTopColors

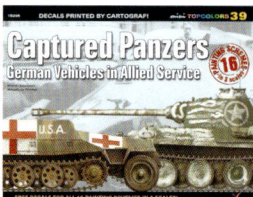

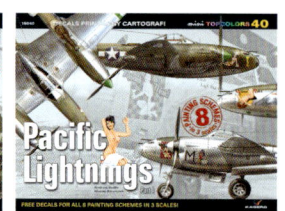

- Fw 190s over Europe
- Captured Panzers – German Vehicles in Allied Service
- Pacific Lightnings

Units

- JG 26 Jagdgeschwader "Schlageter"
- JG 53 "Pik As"

TopDrawings

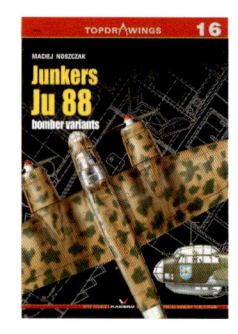

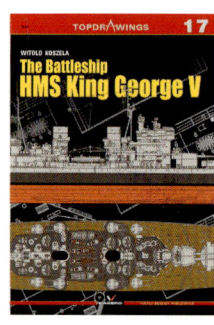

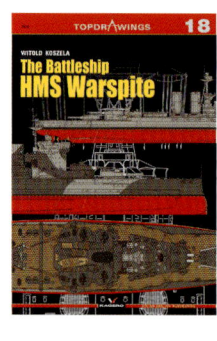

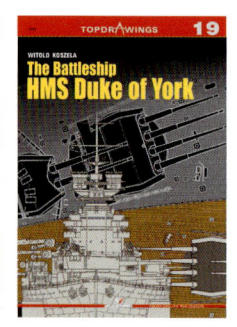

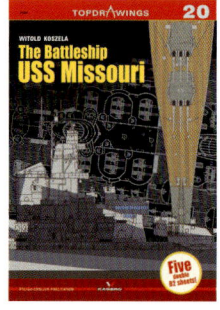

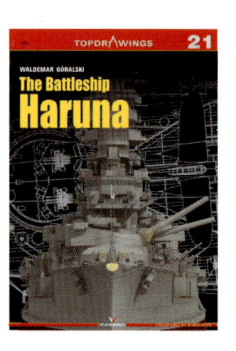

- Junkers Ju 88 bomber variants
- The Battleship HMS King George V
- The Battleship HMS Warspite
- The Battleship HMS Duke of York
- The Battleship USS Missouri
- The Battleship Haruna

Legends of Aviation

- Albatros D.I-D.Va Legendary fighter
- Sopwith Camel

Legends of Aviation in 3D

- Fokker Dr.I The aces' aircraft
- Fokker D.VII The lethal weapon

SuperModel International

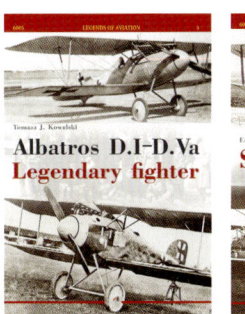

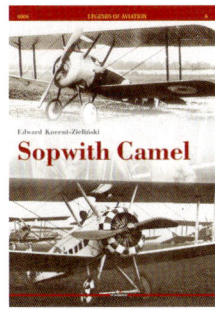

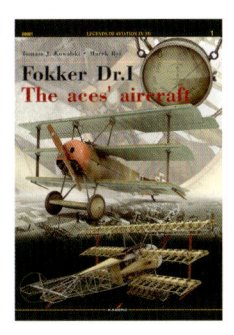

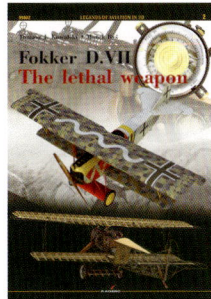

- No.2 SUPERmodel INTERNATIONAL — Jagdpanther / SU-122-54 / Master Box 1:35 BMW R75 / T-55
- No.3 SUPERmodel INTERNATIONAL — Dewoitine D.520 / Hawker Hurricane Mk.I / Spitfire Mk.Vb

SMI Library

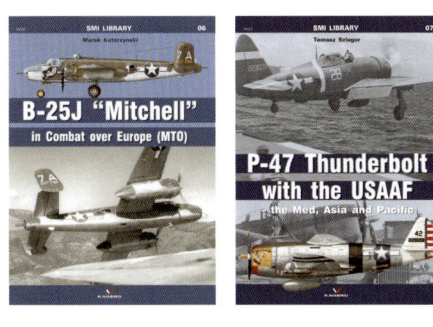

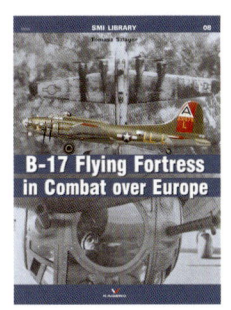

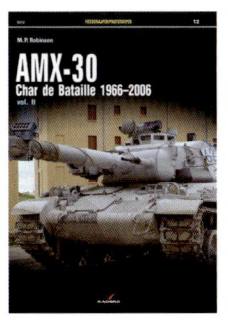

- B-25J "Mitchell" in Combat over Europe (MTO)
- P-47 Thunderbolt with the USAAF the Med, Asia and Pacific
- B-17 Flying Fortress in Combat over Europe

Photosniper

- AMX-30 Char de Bataille 1966–2006
- Sturmgeschütz IV
- Panzerjäger 38(t) Hetzer & G-13 vol. 1

Monographs

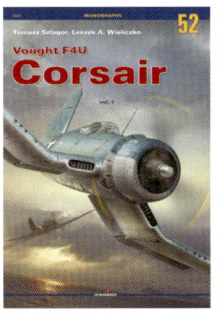

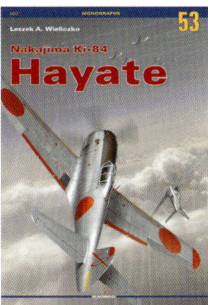

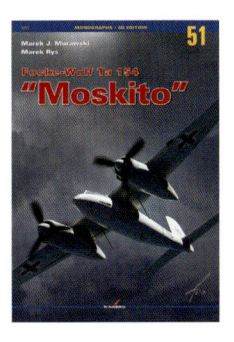

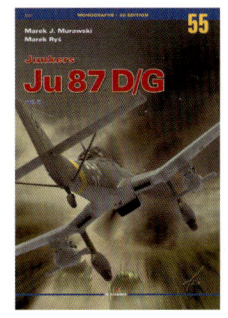

- Vought F4U Corsair
- Nakajima Ki-84 Hayate
- Focke-Wulf Ta 154 "Moskito"

Monographs in 3D

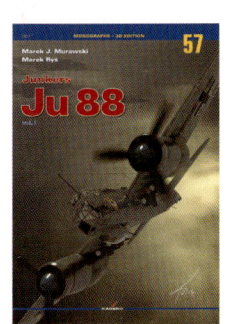

- Junkers Ju 87 D/G
- Junkers Ju 87 D/G
- Junkers Ju 88

Air Battles

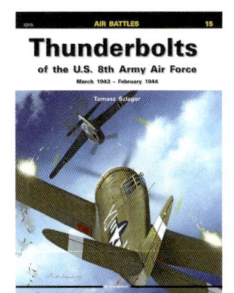

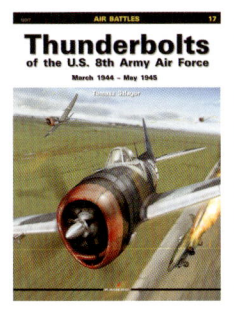

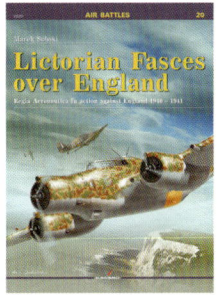

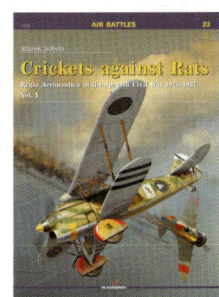

- Thunderbolts of the U.S. 8th Army Air Force March 1943 – February 1944
- Luftwaffe over the desert from January till August 1942
- Thunderbolts of the U.S. 8th Army Air Force March 1944 – May 1945
- Lictorian Fasces over England
- Japanese Fighters in Defense of the Homeland 1941–1944
- Crickets against Rats

Super Drawings in 3D

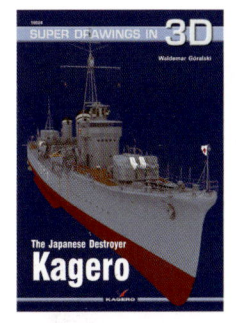

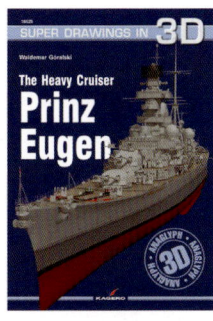

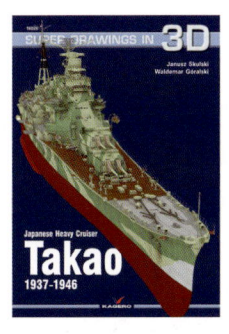

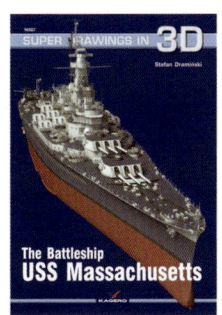

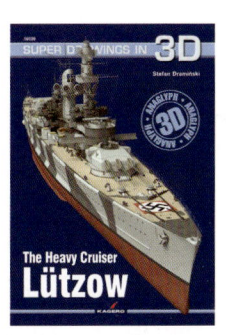

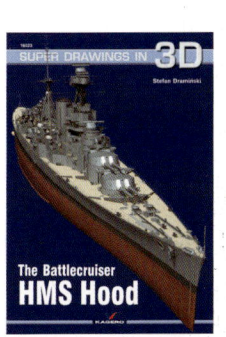

- The Japanese Destroyer Kagero
- The Heavy Cruiser Prinz Eugen
- Japanese Heavy Cruiser Takao 1937-1946
- The Battleship USS Massachusetts
- The Heavy Cruiser Lützow
- The Battlecruiser HMS Hood

www.shop.kagero.pl
phone +4881 501 21 05

Photosniper & Photosniper 3D

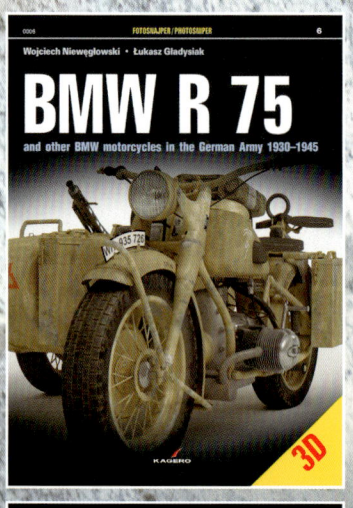

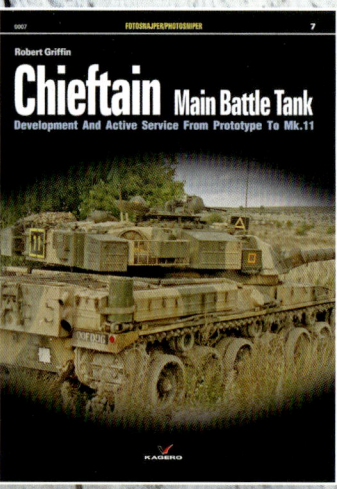

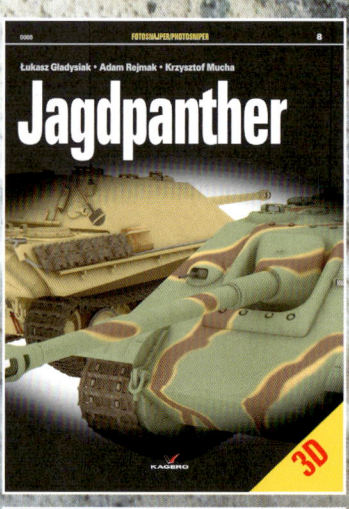

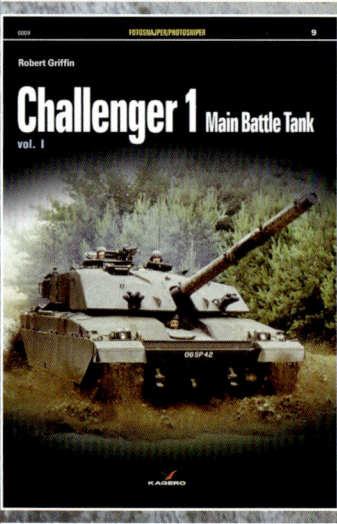

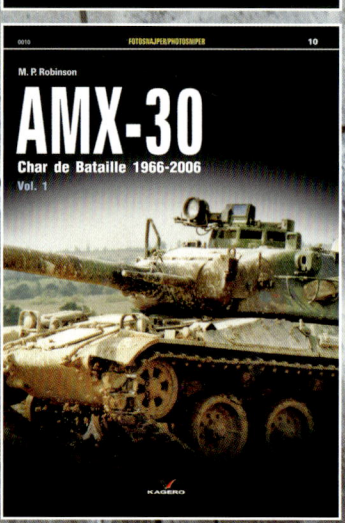

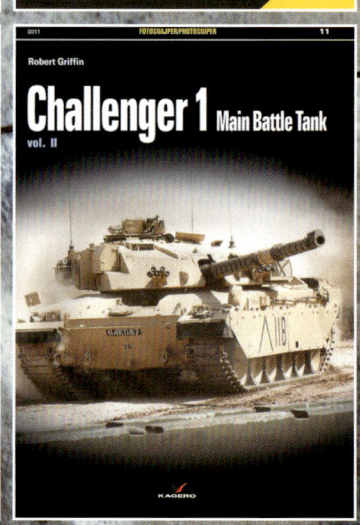

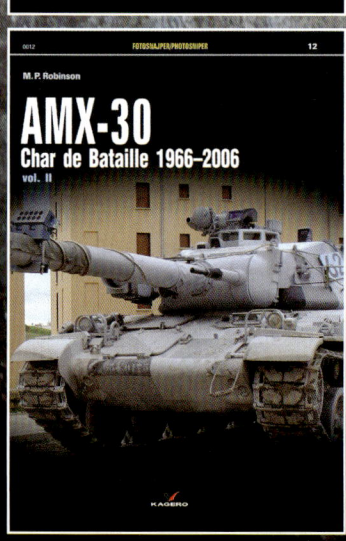

Available on shop.kagero.pl